Contents

Notes on contributors

Alison Clarke-Stewart is Professor of Psychology at the University of California-Irvine.

Philip Hwang is Associate Professor at the Department of Psychology, University of Gothenberg, Sweden

Edward Melhuish is Senior Lecturer at the Department of Psychology, University College of North Wales, and formerly a Senior Research Officer at the Thomas Coram Research Unit, Institute of Education London University.

Peter Moss is Senior Research Officer at the Thomas Coram Research Unit, Institute of Education London University.

Kathy Sylva is Professor of Child Development and Early Education at the Institute of Education London University.

Barbara Tizard is Emeritus Professor at the Institute of Education London University, and formerly Director of the Thomas Coram Research Unit.

Acknowledgements

The papers in this book were presented at a Conference organised by the Thomas Coram Research Unit in February 1990. The Conference organiser, Susan Martin, played a vital role at all stages and the success of the Conference owes a lot to her contribution.

Charlie Owen, at Thomas Coram Research Unit, played an important part in preparing statistical material on services for children under five in Britain.

The proposal for the Conference came from the Department of Health, which also funded the Conference and provided other support throughout the planning and preparation stages.

Introduction

Barbara Tizard

The papers in this book were presented to a two-day conference on Day Care for Under Fives, held at the end of February 1990. The conference was aimed at local authority policymakers and managers of services, and it was concerned both with research findings and with policy issues. In the event, the conference was also attended by representatives of several voluntary societies, and by a number of researchers. It was heavily oversubscribed.

The Department of Health, which funded the conference, asked the Thomas Coram Research Unit to organise it. The Thomas Coram Research Unit has carried out research on services for children under 5 and their families since its inception in 1974. Projects on this topic, funded by the Department of Health, have included studies of the effects on families of making day care centres available, studies of childminding, and of the transition to parenthood. Most recently, we have carried out an important longitudinal study, funded by the Department of Health, which followed the development from infancy until the age of six of children whose mothers returned to full-time work after maternity leave, comparing them with children from similar families whose mothers had decided not to return to work.

One aim of the conference was to present the findings of this project, within the context of similar research from Scandinavia and the USA. From the outset, an international dimension was seen as a crucial aim in discussions of British research and policy, and the papers from Sweden and the USA admirably fulfil that aim. More generally, to its credit, the Department of Health wanted to encourage local authorities to take account of these research findings when planning developments or changes in services for children under 5. Local authority interest in the conference was probably related to two practical considerations. The first of these was the widespread public concern about the lack of day care provision, in the wake of the marked increase in the proportion of women with children under five returning to work. This trend is documented later in the book, and is mirrored in most Western countries. The second consideration was more local. The Children Act, 1989, which will come into force in 1991, places new demands on local authorities with respect to day care. As became obvious during discussion at the conference, local authority managers are very concerned about the way in which the Act will be implemented.

The papers that follow make it clear that earlier anxieties about the damaging effect of day care as such on children have largely been laid to rest. Some researchers, though by no means all, believe that the evidence casts doubt on the wisdom of full-time day care for infants under 12 months; those interested in this hotly contested debate will find it discussed in later chapters. But important though the debate may be, the focus is very narrow and specific – whether children admitted to *full-time* day care (that is, over 20 hours a week) *under 12 months* of age may be at increased risk of developing insecure attachments with their parents.

The view that day care for children *under 3* is necessarily harmful, and that therefore children under this age need full-time parental care, is *not* supported by research. There is ample evidence that good quality day care is not likely to damage, and may benefit, children over one year, especially those from deprived backgrounds. Where detrimental effects are found, they are best explained as due to *poor quality* care, rather than resulting from day care per se. In the Thomas Coram Research Unit longitudinal study, nursery attendance was associated with some restriction on the vocabulary of children aged 18 and 36 months. These children did not come from a deprived background, and nurseries seemed to provide them with less adult-child conversation than was the case with children from a similar background in the care of childminders and relatives. However, these nurseries tended to be under-staffed and poorly resourced. In Sweden, where nurseries are much more generously resourced, it has been established that children in nurseries, at childminders and at home have a similar level of language development, whilst some US studies show intellectual gains for children attending high quality day care centres (see the later chapters by Edward Melhuish, Philip Hwang and Alison Clarke-Stewart).

As Peter Moss, Edward Melhuish and Alison Clarke-Stewart point out, since we know that day care as such is not in itself harmful, the important research questions now are to do with defining, assessing and monitoring quality of care, and, at a more psychological level, with investigating how the child's own characteristics, in terms of age, gender, temperament, and so on, can influence the outcome of different kinds of day care. But it must be acknowledged that all the evidence suggests that high quality day care is very expensive, not least because a high staff-child ratio seems to be a key ingredient. One issue discussed at the conference was whether we should aim to ensure 'good enough' care, i.e. minimum standards to ensure that children are *not harmed* by the experience of day care, or 'high quality' care, which would *enhance all round development*, and thus, as Sylva urges, involve education as well as care. (The founder of the first British nursery school in 1913, Margaret Macmillan, who took children from the age of two, for what is now called 'a long day', insisted that young children need *nurturing*. By this, she meant all round loving care, which would enable them to develop the full range of their abilities.)

But who is to pay for quality care? As Peter Moss and Alison Clarke-Stewart point out, the prevailing British and U S ideology sees childcare as the responsibility (including the financial responsibility) of individual parents, even though they are often unable to pay the cost of quality care. In contrast, as illustrated by Philip Hwang in the case of Sweden, Scandinavian countries view the care of children as in part the responsibility of society as a whole. Hence in Denmark, working parents pay only 25–35 per cent of the cost of childcare, in Sweden, 10–15 per cent. As Peter Moss points out, there are very high, although invisible, costs to the mother for caring for her own children in terms of missed salary, future pension, and so on. And the cost of care outside the home would be even higher if day care staff throughout the world were more adequately paid.

In the early seventies, my late husband, Jack Tizard, took the initiative in establishing two pioneer centres for children under 5, the Thomas Coram Children's Centre and the Dorothy Gardner Centre, where education and care were integrated. He fought for the principle that these Centres, like schools, should be open to all in the neighbourhood, free of charge. The idea seems as visionary and even more unobtainable today as it did twenty years ago. This is because the issue of day care cannot be separated from the wider issues of how we view children and families in relation to the rest of society, and how we, as a relatively rich society, wish to use our resources. These issues may seem academic to those struggling with the day to day problems of coping with existing services, but they underlie the assumptions on which the key decisions are made. For this reason, I believe that the papers in this book will be found stimulating by policymakers, managers and research workers, as well as by practitioners working with young children on a daily basis and by parents.

Policy Issues in Day Care

Peter Moss

Introduction

This chapter sets out some of the main policy issues for day care services in the 1990s. I have tried to avoid suggesting how these policy issues should be resolved, concentrating instead on drawing-up an agenda. This agenda is an international one, in the sense that most of the items upon it are relevant to most developed countries; the chapter also uses a number of foreign examples to illustrate different options.

Any consideration of policy issues in Britain in the 1990s must take account of several developments. Most immediately, there are the issues raised by the implementation of the new Children Act and the potential impact of this legislation on services. Beyond that are the changes occurring in the labour market, particularly the rapid growth in women's employment. By now the figures are well known: two-thirds of labour force growth between 1983 and 1987 consisted of married women, and women are expected to account for over 80 per cent of the anticipated growth between 1987 and 1995 (Department of Employment 1988).

These labour market developments are likely to have a major impact on employment among women with children under 5, one of the main reserves of untapped wage labour. Between 1983 and 1987 alone, before the pace of change had quickened, the proportion of employed women in this group increased from 24 per cent to 35 per cent with, more significantly, the proportion in full-time jobs more than doubling to 11 per cent. Adding a further 7 per cent who were unemployed but seeking work, altogether 42 per cent were economically active by 1987 (OPCS 1989). Looking forward to the latter half of the 1990s, it seems likely that a clear majority of women with pre-school children will be employed, with even more economically active.

The final development is what might be called the European dimension. Being members of a larger European Community has an inevitable influence on expectations and on how, as a society, we think about and tackle various social, economic and environmental issues. More specifically, the European Commission, as part of its Action Programme for the implementation of the Social Charter, is proposing that there should be a Community Recommendation on Childcare. The process of developing that Recommendation and the influence of such a Recommendation once agreed will inevitably broaden and enliven our national debate about day care services.

This chapter focuses particularly on policy issues arising from the increased need for day care services for children with employed parents. In practice, many of the issues cannot be so neatly confined; they apply to the whole range of services for children under five. Moreover, an important issue for the future, discussed further below, is whether we think in terms of separate services for different groups of children – for example, children with parents in full-time jobs – or move to a more integrated approach.

The chapter does not focus on whether or not children under 3 should be in day care – that is no longer an issue for the day care agenda. In practice, some children under 3 have always been in day care, but past policy statements in Britain have suggested that this age group should, in their own interests, be at home with their mothers (for example, Ministry of Health 1968). There is no evidence to support this view. The research debate is now focussed on the comparatively narrow issue of whether or not *full-time* day care for children *under 12 months* may entail some increased risks for *some children*; and the rather broader issue of what conditions in day care for children under 3 may lead to negative or positive outcomes (for a further discussion of these issues, see the later chapters by Edward Melhuish and Alison Clarke-Stewart).

Whether or not the proposition that full-time day care before 12 months entails heightened risk of adverse effects is finally substantiated – and at present it is the subject of great controversy – there is an international trend to introduce Parental Leave extending up to at least the first 12 months after birth. If, as is the case in Sweden, such leave is paid and flexible, to allow part-time working, it will enable parents to make their own choice about the issue as well as to decide how to divide the leave time between mother and father.

In a short chapter, it is impossible to present a comprehensive agenda on day care policy; there are some notable omissions, for example the relationship between parents, workers, service providers and local communities. This chapter concentrates on five main areas – cost, supply, quality, the relationship between services, and the workforce. Though treated under separate headings, in practice these areas are closely inter-related. An American colleague encapsulated one set of relationships when she referred to the 'day care trilemma' – how is it possible to ensure an adequate **supply** of good **quality** day care at a cost that all parents can afford and providing appropriate pay and conditions for **workers?**

Day care policy must also address, for each of these areas, the responsibility and role of three groups – parents, employers and Government at its various levels. Issues about the nature and extent of responsibility must inevitably be based on ideologies. Day care policy in Britain and the United States is heavily influenced by similar dominant ideologies, for example an ideology of 'family life' which emphasises privacy, autonomy and self-sufficiency; children and their care are seen as individual, and more specifically maternal, responsibilities. In other countries, for example in Scandinavia, dominant ideologies place greater emphasis on social solidarity between families with children and the wider society and the consequent sharing of responsibility for children between parents and that wider society. Nor is this necessarily an issue of party political orientation. In France, for example, there is a consensus between Left and Right on the need for public support of families with children, including the provision of assistance with day care services (for a further discussion of this issue, see Melhuish and Moss 1990).

Finally, by way of introduction, one assumption in the chapter should be made clear. I have assumed, and taken as my starting point, that the objective of policy should be to ensure equal access to good quality services to all children whose parents need or want them. While I have assumed this objective, others might object that this underlying concept of 'equality of opportunity' is itself a central and contentious issue, as yet to be agreed. Certainly, it has not been put forward as an explicit objective of current policy, although the statement in April 1989 by the Ministerial Group on Women's Issues might be interpreted as an implicit acceptance of this objective – 'we must ensure that care is of the highest standard and that it gives parents, in both two parent and one parent families, the greatest choice'.

Costs of day care

There are two basic cost questions to be answered. First, what is the real cost of providing good quality day care? The costs of providing non-parental care are both direct (for example, staff pay) and indirect (for example, the cost of various support and supervisory services). The total cost will depend on the assumptions made about both types of cost – for example, what levels of staffing are needed, what constitutes appropriate pay and conditions for day care workers, what support services are needed. Moreover costs, like other aspects of day care, are not static; for reasons discussed below, there is a strong likelihood that costs will need to increase substantially in real terms in the future.

In considering the cost of services, we should remember that providing care for children always involves costs. Full-time maternal care, for instance, imposes very heavy, long-term costs on women due mainly to foregone earnings and consequently reduced pensions (Joshi 1987). Day care services do not therefore involve new costs; rather, they make often invisible costs partially visible, and create the potential for some re-distribution of the costs of caring. The second basic cost question is therefore distributional – how are the costs of non-parental care to be allocated and, in particular, what proportion is to be borne by parents and what proportion by society or employers?

At this point, it is appropriate to introduce a note of caution about the use of the term 'parents'. Research at the Thomas Coram Research Unit shows very clearly that, in Britain at least, day care costs are not usually shared equally between mothers and fathers (just as finding day care and taking children to and from day care are not shared equally); mostly they are treated as the mother's responsibility, to be paid from her earnings, even though they are required because both parents work (Brannen and Moss 1988). Any consideration of the issue of costs therefore must take account of their distribution within as well as without the family.

The proportion of day care costs met by parents varies considerably between countries. This is partly because levels of publicly-funded service vary a lot; in the European Community, for example, Denmark provides such services for nearly half of all children under 3, compared to 2 per cent coverage in the UK (Moss 1988). But there are also differences in the proportion of costs that parents are expected to pay in publicly-funded services. In Sweden, for instance, parents pay between 10–15 per cent, in Denmark between 25–35 per cent. The situation is further complicated because nursery and primary education, which provide day care for many working parents, is free at the time of use, while publicly-funded services for younger children invariably involve a charge on parents.

In most European countries, Governments make some contribution to the day care costs of employed parents, or at least of some employed parents. The UK Government, by contrast, insists that day care for the children of employed parents is a private issue, to be paid for by parents (or, in some cases, by parents and employers). The issue of whether services should be publicly-funded is an ideological matter, based on beliefs about the boundaries of private and public responsibility for children. But there is also a more pragmatic question. Given the high costs involved (see the later chapter by Peter Moss for further discussion of the costs of good quality day care in Britain), given the varying income levels among parents and given the other demands on parents' income – is not some degree of subsidy required to ensure all children equal access to good quality services? And if so, what degree of subsidy is required to achieve this objective?

Where costs are shared by Governments, this can be done through supply subsidy or demand subsidy – that is either by subsidising services directly or by subsidising parents' day care costs through some system of tax relief, vouchers or cash grants. In Sweden, there is political consensus about the need to ensure good quality care for all children, but political disagreement about whether to subsidise services, the course followed so far, or to subsidise parents through cash grants. The United States has a system of tax relief on child care costs, but this is found in only four European Community countries (Belgium, France, Luxembourg, Portugal); these European countries also directly fund care and education services for children under school age, operating in effect a 'mixed' system. During 1989, Belgium introduced a system of tax relief on day costs, while almost at the same time, the Netherlands decided to scrap its system of tax relief and use the money saved to fund a major increase in publicly-funded provision over the next few years.

It is not possible in this chapter to give a thorough review of the pros and cons of supply- or demand-subsidy. The issue is complex, both in principle and practice. To take just two examples: systems of tax relief for daycare costs often favour higher income households (paying higher rates of tax), and preclude the possibility of using public funding as part of an active policy to improve quality or workers' pay and conditions (since tax relief is usually given without conditions); systems of direct funding for services exclude families not able or willing to use such services (for example, because they prefer daycare provided by relatives or because they are unable to obtain a place in a publicly-funded service). The one conclusion that can be drawn is that any decision involving public support for daycare costs, for instance to introduce tax relief, should *not* be considered and taken in isolation from broader considerations about the objectives of policy, the development of services and the overall distribution of costs and benefits.

Because of the role of daycare services in caring for children while parents are at work, should employers be expected or encouraged to subsidise daycare services? This can be done in two ways. In Sweden, all employers contribute towards daycare costs through a payroll levy; Central Government distributes the money to local authorities who, in turn, provide services on a community basis. Employers therefore have a general responsibility, and their contribution is not earmarked for the use of their own workforce; (a somewhat similar system occurs in France, where compulsory employer contributions to 'family allowance funds' (Caisse d'Allocation Familiale) are used increasingly to fund daycare and other childrens services in partnership with local authorities, as well as continuing to provide cash benefits to families with children).

Elsewhere, employers subsidise services on an individual basis. Individual employers (always a small minority of the total; see for example the experience of the USA reported in the later chapter by Alison Clarke-Stewart) decide to make some contribution to daycare for some of their workers. This may be done through direct provision of daycare on-site, subsidising services off-site or subsisiding part of the costs incurred by parents in making their own arrangements.

There are two main issues here. First, if employers are deemed to have some responsibility for daycare, should this be a general and statutory requirement of all employers, as in Sweden; or should individual employers be left to decide whether to initiate policies for members of their own workforce according to their labour force needs? Second, should daycare provision at or near the workplace be encouraged?

The arguments in favour of individual employer and workplace provision are mainly expedient; that is, in the absence of other forms of support for working parents, it is better for a minority of parents to be offered something rather than all parents to be offered nothing. In addition some parents, it is argued, may prefer to have their child cared for near to them at work; unfortunately we have no evidence on parental preferences where the choice is between workplace provision and local provision, both of a comparable standard.

On the other side, there are strong arguments against direct involvement in day care by individual employers – except as a supplement to a system of local services allocated according to the needs of children and their parents. Again, space precludes going into all of these arguments (for a full review of these arguments, see Moss 1990a); let me mention just three. First, it is inappropriate and dangerous to equate day care with other employment perks. Unlike other perks (works canteens, company cars, sports clubs, private health insurance) day care involves the well-being of children. The availability, quality and cost to parents of services for children should not depend on how much an employer values their parents' services, but on the needs of children themselves. Nor should the stability and security of a child's placement depend on whether or not their parents stay with the same employer; this places an unreasonable constraint on parents' choice in a free labour market or exposes children to unnecessary instability of care. Second, services should be available in the neighbourhood where children live, both in the interests of children and parents and of the neighbourhood itself; local services are part of the fabric on which the well-being and cohesion of neighbourhoods depend, and provide one means for the development and maintenance of social networks for parents and children. Finally, the concept of employer provision assumes that services are needed essentially to 'park' children to release parents for employment. If, however, it is accepted that the purpose of services is to benefit children and to provide not only care but education, an issue discussed later, then there is no more reason why employers should be involved in directly subsidising these services than any other service needed for children, such as schools or health clinics.

The issue of employer provision of day care goes to the heart of a central policy issue. Day care services involve a number of interests – children, employers, mothers and fathers – and are relevant to a number of policy areas, including employment, equal opportunities, child welfare and family support. Should employers, whose primary concern must be their labour force needs and economic productivity, be expected to recognise and reconcile these different needs and interests? And if not employers, then whose responsibility is it to take this broad perspective?

The supply of services   The second area for day care policy concerns the supply of services. In particular, to what extent should policy encourage diversity and choice in type of provision and providers of provision? For children under 3, most countries have a mixture of group care and individual care – but should such a mix be encouraged or should only one type be supported? For children over 3, most countries provide a core service of nursery education or kindergarten attended by the great majority of children; working parents supplement this by using some form of out-of-school care. Britain is unusual in having no such general 'core' service; instead there are a number of overlapping services, none of which is dominant in coverage – nursery education, reception classes, playgroups, childminders and day nurseries. Which model do we want for over 3s? And if we maintain the current British approach of a service mix, what should be the role of each service and, an issue discussed further below, what relationship should there be between the different services?

Internationally, there is considerable variation in how publicly-funded services are supplied. In some countries these services are supplied predominantly by local authorities, in others predominantly by private non-profit bodies, which may vary from large organisations to parent groups or worker co-operatives responsible for just one nursery (for a detailed description of the situation in the European Community on this and other aspects of services, see Moss 1988 and 1990b). In Sweden, for example, virtually all publicly-funded services are provided by the local authority; in neighbouring Denmark, however, about half of all services are provided by private organisations but, whether supplied in this way or by local authorities, all services meet similar standards and receive similar levels of public funding. Most countries also have a purely for-profit sector, which receives no direct public funds. However there is no reason why for-profit services should not receive public funds as part of a policy emphasising diversity and choice; an example of this approach is given later.

When considering supply, diversity should not be automatically equated with choice. Because different types of services exist in a country does not automatically mean that a wide choice is equally available to all parents. Diversity is a necessary but not a sufficient condition for choice to exist; other conditions involve availability and the cost of services to parents.

Quality

The third area for day care policy concerns quality. In particular, this raises the question of whether Governments have any responsibility in this area and, if so, whether the responsibility is primarily to protect children from possible harm through enforcing minimum standards for all services or to ensure good quality services for all children. In either case, terms need defining. What harm do we wish to prevent? What do we mean by good quality? The answers to either question are bound to be value-based, reflecting beliefs about what we want or do not want for children, parents, workers and local communities, all of whom need to be considered when attempting to define what we mean by minimum standards or quality. Many people would agree that good quality services should be defined in terms of their ability to facilitate children's development. Even this statement, however, begs several questions, for example what priority should be given to different aspects of development (physical, intellectual, social, emotional, moral, aesthetic and so on)? What types of development do we want to encourage or discourage?

But quality need not only be defined in terms of child development and experiences that enhance development. There are many other parameters which might be considered in

11

attempting to define quality in day care services. Because values and beliefs will vary in a plural society, so too will ideas about the priority to be given to different parameters. We need to explore whether there is an area of shared values in British society, on which base we can build a core area of agreement about quality, while accepting diverse concepts of quality outside this core area; and explore the implications of such diversity.

Once minimum standards or good quality have been defined, it is necessary to identify under what conditions they are most likely to occur, and what actions need to be taken by whom to ensure such conditions. It is important to distinguish *conditions* from the *actions needed to secure them*. Research may, for example, tell us what conditions in a nursery favour the development of particular aspects of good quality; but work then needs to be undertaken to determine what actions are needed to produce most effectively such conditions.

There may well be differences of opinion about what types of action are needed. Some would argue that free market forces, supported perhaps by action to make parents more knowledgeable consumers (for example, through accreditation schemes and information and referral services), provide the most effective strategy to deliver good quality services to all children; others that an interventionist programme of action at local and national levels, planned and co-ordinated by national and local government, is necessary. Later chapters on the situation in Sweden and the United States provide insights into these two strategies; for in the US, there is a heavy emphasis on a free market approach, and improving parents' information, while Sweden has followed a more interventionist approach, with publicly funded services delivered within a very clear framework of government guidelines.

Any discussion of quality needs to take account not only of definition and implementation, but also of access and cost; while already mentioned, this is an important issue that merits restating. The crucial policy questions are – what does good quality care cost? Do we wish to assure access to such care for all children, which means among other things at a price that all parents can afford? How can this be achieved, taking into account differences in the financial and other circumstances of households with children?

The relationship between services

Any discussion of day care services must address the issue of how services providing for children with employed parents should relate to other services for young children. There are two main dimensions to be considered. The first concerns the relationship between care and education. Internationally, the view is gaining ground that quality services for young children must integrate care and education (education being used in its broadest sense of a concern with fostering all aspects of children's development), and by so doing take a comprehensive approach to children's needs. This has led to movements in a number of countries to develop a more educational or pedagogical approach to work with children under 3 in place of what has been traditionally an emphasis on health and physical care.

This change in approach and practice has been matched in some cases by administrative reforms. New Zealand, discussed in more detail later, has explicitly rejected the care/education division in early childhood services and brought all of these services under the responsibility of the Ministry of Education. A major education reform currently being finalised in Spain proposes that all services for children under 6 will become the responsibility of national and regional Education Ministeries, with 0–6 being defined as the first stage of the educational cycle. In Scandinavia, pre-school services have been integrated within Social Welfare Departments, and all share an equal concern with care and education; this is epitomised in the 1987 Pre-School Educational Programme of the Swedish National Board of Health and Welfare, which emphasises that pre-school services have the dual role of fostering the child's development *and* enabling parents to go out to work.

This integrated approach to services for young children also throws into question the very terms commonly used in Britain to describe services – for example 'day care' and 'childcare', with their implied narrow emphasis on 'care'. At present, there is no adequate term in English for services with an integrated approach, 'educare' being a well intentioned but rather inelegant attempt. But in some other countries, alternatives are established or emerging – 'social pedagogy' in Denmark and Sweden, 'acceuil educatif' in France, 'escuela infantile' in Spain.

The relationship between care and education is, of course, a well-established policy issue in Britain, that has been batted around for years. It is particularly problematic and complex in this country. In most countries, most children start nursery school (or its equivalent) at 3 or 4, and have 2 or 3 years of nursery education before starting compulsory schooling; the main care/education divide is between children under and over 3. But in Britain, the divide also affects children over 3 because of the low level of nursery education and the overlapping forms of provision for this age group. As the number of 3 and 4 year old children in private nurseries and with childminders increases, and eventually surpasses the number of children in nursery education, the need to re-assess the theoretical and administrative relationship between care and education will become ever more acute. A further pressure will come from the increasing impact on all under-fives services of recent educational reforms, particularly the National Curriculum and assessment of children at 7 (for a fuller discussion, see the later chapter by Kathy Sylva).

The second dimension in the relationship between day care and other services is the extent to which day care services for children with employed parents should be separated from services for other children. In the U K, children with parents in full-time jobs are cared for by relatives, childminders, nannies and private nurseries; the segregation of this group is increasing with the rapid growth of for-profit and workplace nurseries, quite separate from other types of early childhood service. There are other examples, too, of segregation: public day care services have a heavy concentration of children from disturbed or disadvantaged backgrounds, while playgroups are used disproportionately by middle-class children (Statham et al. 1990). This raises the issue of whether we want to encourage the development of a separate system of services for children with employed parents.

In a number of other countries, steps have been taken which have reduced various forms of segregation. Publicly-funded day care services in many countries traditionally confined their provision to children from poor or disturbed families; in some countries (for example, Denmark and Belgium) there have been moves in recent years to open these services to all employed parents. A similar movement has occurred in Northern Italy, but in the last year or two there has been a supplementary movement to develop the range of services offered in day nurseries, so that they are open not just to all employed parents, but also to other parents and caregivers. Provision of nursery education for all children together with out-of-school care provides an almost universal service for children in many parts of France, whether or not their parents are employed, as does the concept of the 'new school' in the U S (described by Alison Clarke-Stewart in her later chapter).

The relationship between care and education and between services for children with employed parents and other services for young children should be part of a broad policy debate concerning diversity and the relationship between all early childhood services. This needs to identify both the positive and negative features of diversity, and how to enhance the former and reduce the latter; how to clarify the role of, and relationship between, different services; and whether or not a system of diverse services is best served by a coherent national policy framework covering all early childhood services with a lead department responsible for ensuring the implementation of that policy.

The workforce

The final area of daycare policy is the workforce. At one level, this links into the previous issue since changes in the relationship between care and education have implications for workers. For example, more integrated approaches to services often lead to more integrated approaches to training. New Zealand is moving towards a 3 year early childhood training course as the basic qualification for work in all early childhood services. In Spain, teacher training courses specialising in work with under 3s have been developing in recent years. In Denmark, there is a common 3 year course for all workers with children under compulsory school age, with the opportunity to specialise in work with different age groups; pay and conditions are similar whether working with under or over 3s.

Initial training is important. But this is really a part of an issue of more fundamental importance – the conditions required to ensure an adequate supply of workers and to enable them to provide a high quality service. In general, the pay, conditions and status of childcare workers are low, and are lowest among workers with the lowest age group of children (Moss 1988). Some would consider that this was inherently undesirable, reflecting a devaluation of work with children and the way that skilled work done predominantly by women is often treated as if it were unskilled.

There are also more pragmatic concerns. As employment opportunities for women increase, so too does the demand for daycare services. Yet it becomes increasingly difficult to recruit or retain workers for these services. This phenomenon is apparent in a number of countries. In the United States, the National Child Care Staffing Study has covered over 200 daycare centres in 5 major cities (Whitebook et al. 1989). The results just published make grim reading. Turnover among workers in such centres trebled between 1977 and 1988, by which date it had reached an annual rate of 41 per cent. Over this period, earnings actually dropped in real terms; despite having higher levels of formal education than the average American worker, trained daycare workers had 'abysmally low wages', less than half the average earnings for women and a third of the average earnings for men. The report concludes that the most important determinant of staff turnover was staff wages.

The situation is not however confined to America. In Germany, it is proving difficult to recruit nursery workers in big cities, because of high living costs and low wages. Similarly, in Sweden there is a staffing crisis, especially in the Stockholm area, which has affected the opening of new centres and the working of existing ones. For the same reasons, it is also very rare to find either nannies or domestic helps in Sweden or Denmark, indicating how private solutions to the workload in dual-earner households – where high income families buy-in services – become increasingly problematic without a renewable supply of low-wage migrant labour. Within a few years, the servant problem will make one of its regular re-appearances in Britain, as the supply of cheap labour from young women dries up.

Low wages and poor conditions not only cause staffing shortages; they appear to have an adverse effect on the quality of services. The U S National Child Care Staffing Study concludes that 'turnover is detrimental to children'; children attending centres with more staff turnover were less competent in language and social development. Overall, the quality of service provided by most centres was 'barely adequate'; but quality varied widely, and the most important predictor of quality, among the adult work environment variables studied, was staff wages.

Staffing problems are not only restricted to full-time paid workers. In Britain, the playgroup movement is experiencing increasing problems in recruiting volunteers and part-time paid workers both for playgroups and the P P A support network (Statham et al. 1990). While this process is not occurring at the same rate everywhere and can most aptly be described as a process of erosion rather than collapse, it is another indicator of important processes affecting women's willingness and availability to do low paid or unpaid childcare work – or indeed other forms of caring work, for the same processes are at work in other areas.

When thinking about the workforce, we should not forget that the main form of day care for young children with working parents is provided by relatives; indeed this is the case in all Western countries except Denmark and Sweden. The supply of relatives able and willing to provide day care, mostly grandmothers, is unlikely to keep pace with increased demand, and is likely to fall eventually as more female relatives enter the labour market. It should be added that relatives are perhaps the most neglected group of day care workers and have been consistently taken for granted; given their importance, some attention needs to be given to their needs.

One implication of these developments is that over time the cost of day care services (and indeed of all human services) will have to increase substantially, both to ensure a sufficient supply of workers and as a condition for the development of high quality services. This will be part of the process by which the subsidy of childcare costs, provided by non-employed mothers and low paid workers, is gradually removed. The issue of childcare workers also illustrates the dynamic and far-ranging effects of women with young children entering the labour force in large numbers. Because of this, and the crucial importance of childcare workers to quality, it is essential for somebody, and it is difficult to see who else this can be but Government, to take a strategic role in forward planning to secure an adequate workforce and to develop conditions which will optimise their work; this in turn brings the discussion back full circle to questions about the cost of good quality day care and its allocation.

Different models

This book contains chapters about the United States and Sweden, which offer very different models for organising day care services. The former like Britain emphasises the private market, with a restricted public sector mainly for children with high social need; the latter emphasises public funding and provision of services. A third mode is provided by New Zealand where a mixed system is developing, combining public funding with mainly private provision (for a fuller discussion of the situation in New Zealand, see Working Party on Early Childhood Care 1988, Burns 1989). New Zealand, like the UK, has a diversity of services provided by a variety of private and public suppliers; a 1988 Government Working Group identified over 20 types of early childhood service, ranging from childminders to playgroups and from day care centres to kindergartens, and which received funding in various ways from a diversity of sources and at different levels.

As part of a major reform of the education service all early childhood services have been made the responsibility of the Ministry of Education; 'New Zealand no longer makes the distinction between care and education (recognising) that the younger the child the more impossible it is to separate these two components' (Burns 1989). This administrative reform has only been the starting point. The Government is committed to increasing public funding for all types of early childhood services so that all are funded on the same basis and at the same level as the best funded service, kindergartens. However all services wishing to receive these funds must sign an agreement with the Ministry of Education; the agreement requires the service to have a charter, developed in consultation with parents and workers, which shows how the service will meet new national guidelines.

The New Zealand reform is based on a clear Government commitment to provide equal access for all children to good

17

quality care and education services. The Government has assumed responsibility for most of the costs, partly to ensure that all services are 'affordable' to all parents and so equally accessible, and public funds are used as part of a strategy to improve quality. As well as taking responsibility for the quality of all funded services, the Government has set minimum standards for non-funded services, all of which must be registered. It has not however assumed responsibility for supply; publicly funded services will be under a variety of managements, including local authorities, but mostly voluntary bodies and private entrepreneurs. Moreover it is deliberately sustaining diversity in types of provision, by applying its policy framework to every kind of early childhood service, including childminders, playgroups, kindergartens and day care centres. In short, New Zealand offers a model of a 'mixed economy' of services, with access and quality underwritten by public funds.

Conclusion

Over the next year, the main policy issues in Britain will be concerned with the new Children Act, in particular the content of the associated regulations and guidelines and the way that regulatory powers will be applied. The Act is an important development, as are some other Government initiatives, for example the Rumbold Committee. But they are only a starting point. As a society, we have yet to draw up the full policy agenda, let alone begin to work through that agenda in an open-minded, thorough and thoughtful way, which recognises the profundity and inter-connectedness of the issues facing us concerning childhood and the upbringing of children, the relationship between employment, parenthood and gender equity and the allocation of work and cost across the whole field of caring work.

As we enter the 1990s and move through a period of rapid change, much more is needed. In particular, the time is right for the preparation of a new policy statement on early childhood services, covering care and education for children under 5 and out-of-school provision for older children. A review of existing policy and of future policy options should form part of the process of preparing this policy statement. This process should also provide an invaluable opportunity to involve the various interested parties – parents, employers, researchers, different groups of workers, policy-makers and politicians – and to seek a consensus based on a shared understanding of the issues involved and a shared commitment to providing the best solutions for all our children and their parents.

References

Brannen, J. and Moss, P. (1988). *New Mothers at Work.* London: Unwin Hyman.

Burns, V. (1989). *Early Childhood Education in New Zealand – the Quiet Revolution.* Paper given to the O M E P X I X World Assembly, London University, July 1989.

Department of Employment (1988). *Employment for the 1990s.* London: HMSO.

Joshi, H. (1987). 'The cost of caring'. In C. Glendinning and J. Millar (eds.) *Women and Poverty in Britain.* Brighton: Wheatsheaf.

Lloyd, E., Statham, J., Moss, P., Melhuish, E. and Owen, C. (1990). *Playgroups in a Changing World.* London: HMSO.

Melhuish, E. and Moss, P. (eds.) (1990). *Day Care for Young Children: International Perspectives.* London: Routledge.

Ministry of Health (1968). *Circular 37/68.*

Moss, P. (1988). *Childcare and Equality of Opportunity.* Brussels: European Commission.

Moss, P. (1990a). 'Work, family and the care of children: issues of equality and responsibility'. *Children and Society, 4*, 2, 145–166.

Moss, P. (1990b). *Childcare in the European Community, 1985–1990.* Brussels: European Commission.

OPCS (1990). *General Household Survey 1987.* London: HMSO.

Whitebook, M., Howes, C. & Phillips, D. (1989). *Who Cares? Child Care Teachers and the Quality of Care in America: Executive Summary of the National Child Care Staffing Study.* Oakland: Child Care Employee Project.

Working Group on Early Childhood Care and Education (1988). *Education to be More.* Wellington NZ: Government Printer.

Research Issues in Day Care
Edward Melhuish

Does day care affect young children?

Early research on day care focused on the question: is day care bad for young children? Attitudes to such a question were heavily influenced by the work of John Bowlby on the infant's needs for and attachment to the mother and the potential risks of separation from the mother. As experience accumulated that day care does not necessarily have detrimental effects for children, this question ceased to be topical (see Tizard 1986 for fuller discussion). In recent years though, it has re-emerged on the day care research agenda, specifically with regard to children in the first year of life; I shall return to this specific issue later as part of a discussion of the relationship between day care and children's age.

Despite this recent re-emergence, albeit in a relatively limited form, of the controversy about whether or not day care per se may be harmful to children, over the years research has been increasingly concerned with identifying what specific aspects of *children's experience* have implications for their well-being and development and which factors or conditions in the *care environment* are most likely to foster developmentally beneficial experiences. Before considering this research, two general points should be stressed. First, the issue of experience and environment is relevant to development whether care is provided in the child's home with mother, father or nanny, in another person's home with a relative or a childminder, or in a nursery or day care centre. Second, the effects that care settings may produce can be positive or negative. Indeed, the same care environment may produce a positive effect for one aspect of development and a negative effect for another aspect of development: for example, a heavily structured educationally-oriented nursery may well improve reading readiness but may not facilitate independence in the child.

Quality of day care

The issue of quality arises regularly in any debate about day care. But what do we mean by quality of day care? The terms 'good quality' and 'bad quality' care are often used as if the dimension of quality was one dimensional, with a high point and low point; the assumption is that all care settings can be placed somewhere on a line joining these two points. However, it may be better to consider quality of care along several dimensions, so that any given care setting may be high on one dimension, low on a second and middling on a third.

Any approach to the issue of quality will start from and involve value judgements – we are being asked to decide what we think is good or bad, desirable or undesirable. There is also the question of quality for whom – children, parents, child care workers. Different perspectives raise different criteria.

On what basis should we define quality? One approach is to focus on the child's experience, and the extent to which that experience enhances or hinders the child's development. In short, this approach defines quality of care in terms of child development. Good quality care is that care which is developmentally beneficial, while bad quality is that care which inhibits development. Most research on quality has been explicitly or implicitly guided by this approach, and I shall return to consider this research. But first I want to consider an alternative approach, which defines quality in terms of rights.

Defining quality in terms of children's rights

From almost any perspective children would be regarded as having the right to an environment which enables them to achieve their potential and which, therefore, facilitates development. Hence an approach based upon children's rights would certainly encompass all the factors included in the definition based upon child development. However depending upon the values held by society the child may be regarded as having rights which go beyond the provision of an environment which can be empirically demonstrated to facilitate development. An example might be the right to cared for as part of a community which values the religious, ethnic and racial identity of the child. The justification for the awarding of such a right would be in terms of fostering the child's sense of identity. In that children's sense of identity is a fundamental aspect of their development, such a right could well be included within a definition based upon the facilitation of child development.

Other examples of rights that might be assigned to children include the right to health, individuality, respect, dignity, opportunities for learning and socializing with adults and children, freedom from discrimination such as racism or sexism and cultural diversity. The extent to which a day care setting fulfils these rights may be used in defining the quality of care for that setting.

All of the above rights can be regarded as potentially contributing to children's physical, intellectual, social or emotional development. For some of these rights there exists research evidence specifying the details of the relationship between the experience of the rights and subsequent development. For example the right to a stable learning and caring environment can be specified in terms of which details of that environment will facilitate which aspects of intellectual, linguistic or social development. For other rights such as the right to cultural diversity the details of the appropriate childcare practices for different age groups for facilitating the child's sense of self and appreciation of cultures can be guessed at but as yet await empirical evidence.

Where justification for children's rights does not rest upon the implications for children's development, then empirical evidence may not be needed or even desired as the right is seen as inherent, without need for further justification. Alternatively the right may be seen as reflecting values which are automatically accepted within a society. An advantage of an approach based on self-evident rights is that there is no need to be limited by the availability of empirical evidence, which is also the main disadvantage as the best way to enact a right often needs empirical verification.

Definitions in terms of parental rights

The approaches so far considered have been child-centred. However it may well be appropriate to include certain parental rights within a definition of quality of childcare. One reason for this is to enable parents to influence the nature of their children's care environments. To this end, it would be necessary to consider whether day care settings offered parents the opportunity to:

1. acquire information about the care environment;

2. express their viewpoint on the care environment;

3. actually alter the care environment of their child;

4. contribute to their child's care environment;

5. choose between alternative childcare environments.

Another reason for including parental rights would be to enable parents to have some choice in how to divide their time between parenting and other activities. For this purpose questions about parents' access to day care services, choice between services, transport to services and hours that childcare is available become relevant.

Definitions in terms of childcare workers rights

Workers play a crucial role in day care services. The characteristics of day care environments will be dramatically influenced by the characteristics of the workers, and conversely the workers themselves will be affected by the environments in which they work. There are therefore good grounds for including the rights of childcare workers in a consideration of the quality of daycare.

One approach considers how staffing characteristics affect children's experiences and there is some research evidence available linking staffing and children's experience and development, which is considered below. Another approach is to consider the rights of the worker as an employee and the extent to which employment rights are met within a particular setting.

Research on quality of care

Research has primarily started from the perspective that good quality care is that care which is developmentally beneficial. Research on child development points to several aspects of the young child's experience as having potential developmental consequences (e.g. Phillips 1987). Taking this perspective, these aspects of experience should be regarded as equivalent to the quality of care.

Adult-child relationships are crucial. There are several studies both in home and day care settings which reveal positive developmental benefits associated with aspects of adult-infant interaction, notably affection and sensitive responsiveness between adult and child (for example, Clarke-Stewart 1973, Ainsworth et al. 1978, Carew 1980, McCartney 1984, Goelman and Pence 1987). 'Sensitive responsiveness' refers to the likelihood of a child's communication receiving an appropriate response. Children enrolled in day care with more responsive caregivers are likely to have better cognitive and language development (Carew 1980, Rubenstein and Howes 1983, Melhuish et al. 1990) and also to be more socially competent (Rubenstein and Howes 1983).

Research in home environments has found that responsive interaction between parents and children also fosters secure attachments (Ainsworth et al. 1978), and it seems likely that similar processes will operate in day care. There is accumulating evidence that secure attachment relationships between children and their caregivers are associated with a wide range of developmental advantages. Where a warm secure relationship exists between an adult and child, the child is better able to use the adult to explore the environment. This is true in the home (Ainsworth et al. 1978), while in day care settings more securely attached caregivers fulfil this function more often than insecurely attached caregivers (Cummings 1980). Toddlers show different patterns of social interaction with stable than with less stable caregivers (Rubenstein and Howes 1983). Young children learning to communicate will often use idiosyncratic speech or gestures; a caregiver who is familiar with a child is likely to learn such idiosyncrasies and be able to respond quickly and appropriately, whereas a new caregiver is more likely to fail to understand the communication and thus be unable to show sensitive responsivity.

Peer relationships are also important. Where children have more experience of peer interaction, their skills in such interaction improve (for example, Mueller and Brenner 1977, Field et al. 1984). There is ample evidence that the social skills of pre-school children are facilitated by group experience in a variety of sessional and full-time day care settings (Clarke-Stewart 1987, Howes 1988, Melhuish 1990). In peer relationships, prosocial and sophisticated role playing proceed better between good friends (for example, Young and Lewis 1979, Stefani and Camaioni 1983). Same-age and mixed-age groups supply useful and complementary forms of experience, and if children can experience both sorts of group that will probably be beneficial.

Good learning opportunities provide developmentally important experience. Young children are continuously learning about the environment and people around them. The way in which their experiences are structured will affect how this learning progresses and what is learnt. Sometimes learning opportunities are explicitly planned for, but often they are inherent in the daily activities of the children. Children will obviously benefit more from environments which provide the most appropriate learning opportunities. Indeed they are likely to become bored and possibly upset in situations which are unstimulating. There are several relevant strands of research, for example the work in Sweden by Sundell (1988) showing how the amount and kind of instruction available in pre-school services affects children's communicative and cognitive competence; and the research undertaken in East Germany on the benefits of different ways of introducing new activities to children which illustrates the advantages of scheduling activities to fit children's developmental level (Weigl and Weber 1990).

The importance of *health and safety* is obvious. A child who is made sick or injured by its surroundings is not benefitting from them. Also a hazardous environment will lead caregivers to be concerned with the avoidance of possible hazards and not with optimising the experiences of children. In such a situation, caregivers are likely to be highly controlling, so limiting the exploration of children which is a basic mechanism of learning.

Finally, it is important for children to *enjoy their care setting*; children should be happy. Often this aspect of children's experience, which is perceived as obviously important by childcare workers, is overlooked in research. The justification for emphasizing such an aspect of care can be made perfectly adequately on humanitarian grounds, regardless of research.

There is however research evidence that the learning of new concepts proceeds more efficiently when children are in a 'happy' emotional state. Unhappy children do not explore their environments and will often cut themselves off from the outside world. All children are individuals and have their own personalities. However, in general, when children are happy their interactions with adults will occur with reasonable frequency and will tend to be characterized by positive emotional reactions. Conversely, unhappy children will show reduced levels of interaction, with predominantly negative reactions to others. Levels of cooperation will increase when children are happy, and confrontational situations will be reduced. Hence, communication proceeds more effectively when children are in a happy state of mind, and the benefits of all kinds of interaction are likely to be increased when the emotional climate is favourable. There is plenty of scope for the development of appropriate measures in this area – of indicators of 'happiness' – as part of the broader development of measures of the quality of children's experience.

Conditions that contribute to positive experiences

Research has identified a number of conditions or factors which are likely to contribute to positive experiences and good developmental outcomes – although they do not guarantee them.

In the structuring of day care settings, *group size* is an important factor. Generally small groups do better (Ruopp et al. 1979), being related to positive outcomes for a wide range of developmental indicators. The size of group which is most beneficial will change with the age of the children. Infants generally need smaller groups than two to four year old children.

Group size needs to be considered in conjunction with *adult:child ratios*. Here again, the age of children is relevant; as the age of children increases, and particularly as their independence and capacity for peer interaction develops, then the ratio may be increased substantially. For the youngest age groups, however, ratios should be low. For children under 18 months, it is difficult for one adult to provide sensitive individual care for more than three children; the demands of caretaking, feeding, cleaning and changing alone can take up all the caregiver's time, with greater numbers of infants leaving no spare capacity for responsive attention. In the 18–30 month age range, Dutch research suggests that interaction deteriorates rapidly as the ratio goes above 1:5 (Smeets and Goossens 1988). Consideration may also need to be given to how caregivers are deployed during the day, within these overall averages. Are there times in each day when low adult:child ratios exist in order to enable adult-child interaction on a one to one basis?

If so, then substantially higher ratios may apply for other parts of the day.

Day care is very labour-intensive, and the workforce play a crucial role in determining children's experience. Quantity, as expressed in adult:child ratios is an important factor, but there are other equally important considerations. American, French and Israeli research find benefits from extra *staff training* (Lezine 1974, Howes 1983, Rosenthal 1990). For example, mothers are usually good at providing sensitive responsiveness without any special training, but the difference in the emotional commitment to the child between caregivers and the mother means that such responsiveness may not develop so readily for caregivers. While to some degree sensitive responsiveness will reflect personality characteristics, appropriate training can help to improve responsiveness for most caregivers (Howes 1983). Training can also make caregivers more aware of stages in children's development and the need to adjust to the child's changing developmental needs. Skill in structuring peer interaction situations is more likely to foster competence and caregiver training has been associated with more competent peer interaction for two-year-olds (Howes and Unger 1989).

As already mentioned, *stability of caregivers* is likely to contribute to more positive experiences for children, increasing responsivity and secure attachments. The importance of stability as a condition that favours good experience and positive developmental consequences is emphasised by the results from the National Day Care Staffing Study (Whitebrook et al. 1989). This large-scale American study reports a clear relationship between turnover, day care environments and children's development, with poorer environments and poorer language and social development associated with higher staff turnover.

There are two main aspects of stability of care. One concerns the continuity of the care placement (how long a child remains in the same placement), and the other concerns the stability of caregivers within a placement. For both, a limited amount of instability is probably of little consequence, but beyond some low threshold instability is likely to be detrimental for the child's experience. It is also possible that stability may be more important with younger children when the establishment of stable interpersonal relationships and the development of communication skills are more vulnerable; as already noted, the highly idiosyncratic communications of young children often require an adult with considerable knowledge of the child for appropriate interpretation and response (Melhuish et al. 1990).

What conditions are likely to favour caregiver stability? The National Child Care Staffing Study emphasises the importance of *pay and other employment benefits;* staff wages were the most important determinant of turnover. The availability of alternative employment opportunities and the general state of the labour market are also likely to be important and to interact with pay and conditions. Where pay and conditions are poor, and other employment possibilities exist, then problems of recruitment and turnover will increase.

A final factor affecting caregivers is the *level of other demands* made on them, over and above working with children. American research (Howes 1983) finds poorer adult-infant interaction where high housework demands are placed on staff; such demands will obviously limit the capacity and time for caregivers to interact with children. Non-child demands are always likely to be present to some degree, but careful attention needs to be paid to getting a satisfactory balance between these demands and purely child-related demands made of staff.

Finally, levels of *equipment and accommodation* are important conditions affecting experience. Inadequate equipment generally limits the activities that are available, and more specifically precludes the possibility of an extensive curriculum of activities. Bad accommodation can create health and safety hazards, hamper the ability of staff to apply good practice and again limit the activities available to children.

These factors are important not only because they are likely to affect children's experience in day care, and therefore the consequences for them of attendance, but also because they can be made subject to regulation and are readily amenable to change. There already exist a variety of checklists and rating scales covering these factors, which have been primarily used by researchers, and there is extensive scope for developing such measures to suit the needs of practitioners. This provides a promising area for co-operation between practitioners and researchers.

The relationship between home care and day care

In assessing the impact of day care on children's development, it is important to remember that day care is not their only significant care environment; even children in full-time day care spend a lot of time at home and their development will be shaped by both environments and the relationship between them. This relationship is represented in Figure 1. When the quality of care in both settings is equivalent or balanced, then there is likely to be little effect from attending day care. Where quality of care in day care is superior in some significant respects to the home, then children receiving day care are likely to show positive or beneficial effects, as seen in several studies of children from disadvantaged families receiving good quality day care (for example, Golden et al. 1978, Ramey and Mills, 1977, O'Connell and Farran, 1982). However, where the quality of out-of-home care is inferior to that of the home care available, then negative or detrimental effects may occur, as reported in at least one study in both.the U S A and the U K (Desai et al. 1989, Melhuish et al. 1990).

Figure 1

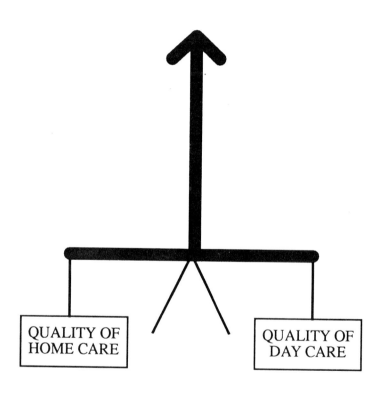

EFFECTS OF DAY CARE

NEGATIVE - - - -NEUTRAL - - - - -POSITIVE

QUALITY OF HOME CARE

QUALITY OF DAY CARE

Hence both positive and negative effects for day care are to be expected as a function of the relationship between home care and day care, with no day care effects where there is approximate equivalence in quality of care in the settings. A corollary of this point is that the same day care may have different effects for different groups of children depending upon the relative quality of home care available.

Children's age and day care

How old should young children be before experiencing substantial amounts of day care? A common approach to the issue has been to rely upon the theoretical perspectives of John Bowlby's early writings (Bowlby 1953) which stressed the importance of the first three years for maintaining the stability of the mother-child relationship, and the need to avoid day care during this period. However, there have been ample demonstrations that children can spend much of their lives in non-parental care in the first three years without negative consequences.

Although the general proposition that children should receive full-time parental care for their first three years is no longer sustainable, the issue has re-emerged in a very modified form in recent years. Belsky (1988) has put forward the proposition that children who start *full-time* day care (defined as more than 20 hours a week) before *12 months of age* are at *increased risk* of forming an insecure attachment to the mother. As attachment to the mother is claimed to mediate several developmental processes, Belsky further argues that early full-time day care may produce an increased risk of certain long-term detrimental effects, particularly for social and emotional development, leading for example to an increased likelihood of certain types of problematic behaviour in children of primary school age.

This proposition has caused much controversy and is hotly disputed. A number of questions have been raised about Belsky's conclusions:

Is the claimed association between day care and insecure attachment due to day care itself or is it a 'spurious relationship' in which insecure attachment is the product of factors associated with day care use rather than day care itself (for example, that users of day care for very young children have certain characteristics that increase the likelihood of insecure attachment)? Are the procedures for measuring attachment equally appropriate for both children who are in full-time parental care at home and children who use day care?

Does the association with longer term development in fact exist?

These questions have been raised in a number of recent papers (for example, Clarke-Stewart 1988, Richters and Zahn-Waxler 1988, and Thompson 1988), and are discussed further in the later chapter by Alison Clarke-Stewart on American day care provision and research. In Sweden, the issue has become irrelevant in practice with the introduction of a generally used entitlement to 12 months paid parental leave, discussed further in Philip Hwang's chapter (though it is worth noting that earlier Swedish research on children admitted to day care before 12 months of age has shown no evidence of adverse effects).

The increasing availability of parental leave entitlements in developed countries, which offer mothers or fathers the opportunity to take full-time or part-time leave during the first 12 months after birth, will make the 'Belsky debate' more a matter of theoretical than practical interest over time. However, for other reasons children's age remains a critical variable in considering day care. In particular, the needs of children change as they get older and move through different stages of development, and day care settings need to take account of this, creating age-appropriate environments and experiences. The implications of this for adult:child ratios have already been mentioned, but the age factor is important in other respects, for example the structuring of groups for facilitating social experience as well as the provision of appropriate learning opportunities for children. More generally, the formulation of regulations and guidance for day care services should take account of the different requirements of children at different ages, and training in childcare should comprehensively deal with the changing pattern of children's needs as they develop.

Education and care

The distinction between education and care is not clear-cut, and the younger the child the more difficult it becomes to make a distinction between the functions of education and care. A number of countries, for example Sweden and New Zealand, have rejected the distinction, both organisationally (by integrating all early childhood services within one Government department) and conceptually (by defining services as having both a care and educational or pedagogical role). Such developments raise important policy issues, but also important research issues. What does education for children under 3 mean? What are the implications of introducing an educational orientation in all services for young children from babies upwards? What conditions are most likely to foster such an orientation?

These broad issues about the relationship between care and education are of international concern. More specifically in a British context is the issue of the implications of recent educational reform, especially the introduction of the National Curriculum and assessment of children at age 7, on pre-school services. Related to this is the possible consequence for later educational attainment of children whose experience of preschool day care differs. To the extent that the quality of care may affect the development of children such effects may be reflected in differences in educational attainment. These issues will be discussed further in the later chapter by Kathy Sylva.

Conclusion

Since the War, research on day care has moved away increasingly from asking whether or not day care, in itself, is bad for children. With the exception of the important, but limited, 'Belsky' debate, that issue has now run its course. The emphasis now is on gaining understanding, both of theoretical and practical value, of conditions and factors in day care which enhance children's well-being. Similarly, debates about the relevant pros and cons of group care versus childminding are giving way to an interest in how to enhance each type of care, to provide parents with a real choice of good quality provision. Even the 'Belsky' debate emphasises this process of seeking specific conditions, for Belsky's proposition about the harmful effects of early day care is presented in terms of very specific conditions, so that for example part-time day care for children under 12 months is not deemed problematic.

This chapter has concentrated on research issues concerning children in general, and it should be recognised that there are other specific research issues that require attention. Research attention needs to be paid to specific groups of children, for example those from ethnic minorities and those with special needs. The US National Child Care Staffing Study illustrates how research on childcare workers, and their conditions, is important in its own right, but also has a direct bearing on children's well-being. There are also important research issues concerning parents and day care, including the relationship between parents and day care services, and parental needs and preferences for services. At a time when day care is of increasing importance in Britain, a review of day care policy, such as was proposed in the previous chapter, should be matched by a review of research needs in a British context, leading to a broad, long-term programme of work based on close collaboration between researchers, practitioners and policy-makers.

References

Ainsworth, M., Blehar, M., Walters, E. & Wall, S. (1978). *Patterns of attachment*. Hillsdale, NJ: Erlbaum.

Belsky, J. (1988). 'The "effects" of infant day care reconsidered.' *Early Childhood Research Quarterly*, 3, 235–272.

Bowlby, J. (1953). *Child care and the growth of love*. London: Penguin.

Carew, J. V. (1980). 'Experience and development of intelligence in young children at home and in day care'. *Monographs of the Society for Research in Child Development, 45 (6–7, serial No. 187)*.

Clarke-Stewart, K. A. (1973). 'Interactions between mothers and their young children'. *Monographs of the Society for Research in Child Development, 38, (6–7. Serial No. 153)*.

Clarke-Stewart, K. A. (1987). 'Predicting child development from child care forms and features: The Chicago study.' In D. A. Phillips (Ed.) *Quality in child care: What does research tell us?* Washington, D.C.: National Association for the Education of Young Children.

Clarke-Stewart, A. (1988). 'The "effects" of infant day care reconsidered: Risks for parents, children, and researchers.' *Early Childhood Research Quarterly*, 3, 293–318.

Cummings, E. H. (1980). 'Caregiver stability and day care'. *Developmental Psychology, 16*, 31–37.

Desai, S., Chase-Lansdale, P. L. & Michael, R. T. (1989). 'Mother or market? Effects of maternal employment on the intellectual ability of four-year-old children.' *Demography*.

Field, T., Vega-Lahr, N., & Jagadish, S. (1984). 'Separation stress of nursery school infants and toddlers graduating to new classes.' *Infant Behavior and Development, 7*, 227–284.

Goelman, H. & Pence, A. R. (1987). 'Effects of child care, family, and individual characteristics on children's language development: The Victoria day care research project.' In D. A. Phillips (ed.) *Quality in child care: What does research tell us?* National Association for the Education of Young Children: Washington, D.C.

Golden, M., Rosenbluth, L., Grossi, M., Policare, H., Freeman, H. & Brownlee, M. (1978). *The New York Infant Day Care Study*. Medical and Health Research Association of New York city, NY10013.

Howes, C. (1983). 'Caregiver behavior In center and family day care.' *Journal of Applied Developmental Psychology, 4,* 99–107.

Howes, C. (1988). 'Peer Interaction in young children'. *Monographs of the Society for Research in Child Development. 53 (1, Serial No. 217).*

Howes, C., & Unger, O. (1989). 'Play with peers in childcare settings.' In M. Block & A. Pelllgrini (eds) *The Ecological Context of Children's Play.* Norwalk, NJ.: Ablex.

Lezine, I. (1974). *Propos sur le jeune enfant.* Paris: Mame.

McCartney, K. (1984). 'Effects of quality of day care environment on children's language development.' *Developmental Psychology, 20,* 244–260.

Melhuish, E. C., Lloyd, E., Martin, S. & Mooney, A. (1990). 'Type of day care at 18 months: II Relations with cognitive and language development' *Journal of Child Psychology and Psychiatry, 31.*

Melhuish, E. C. (1990). 'Research on day care for young children in the United Kingdom.' In E. C. Melhuish and P. Moss (eds) *Day care for young children: International perspectives.* London: Routledge.

Mueller, E. & Brenner, J. (1977). 'The origins of social skills and interaction among playgroup toddlers.' *Child Development, 48,* 854–861.

O'Connell, J. C. & Farran, D. C. (1982). 'Effects of day care experience on the use of Intentional communicative behaviors in a sample of socio-economically depressed infants.' *Developmental Psychology, 18, 22–29.*

Phillips, D. A. (ed.) (1987). *Quality in child care: What does research tell us?* Washington, D.C.: National Association for the Education of Young children.

Ramey, C. T. & Mills, P. (1977). 'Social and intellectual consequences of day care for high-risk Infants.' In R. Webb (Ed.) *Social development in childhood: Daycare programs and research.* Baltimore: John Hopkins University Press.

Rosenthal, M. (1990). 'Social policy and its effects on the daily experiences of infants and toddlers in family day care in Israel.' *Journal of Applied Developmental Psychology, 11,* 85–103.

Richters, J., & Zahn-Waxler, C. (1988). 'The infant day care controversy: Current status and future directions.' *Early Childhood Research Quarterly, 3,* 319–336.

Rubenstein, J. L., and Howes, C. (1983). 'Socio-emotional development of toddlers in day care: The role of peers and individual differences.' In S. Kilmer (Ed.) *Advances in Early Education and Day Care.* San Francisco: JAI Press.

Ruopp, R., Travers, J., Glantz, F. & Coelen, C. (1979). *Children at the center: Final results of the national day care study.* Cambridge, MA: Abt Associates.

Smeets, H. & Goossens, F. A. (1988). 'Kwaliteit van de Interactie en stafkInd ratio: Verslag van een voorondettoek.' *Informatiebulletin voor Ontwikkelingsychologie, 15,* 11–122

Stefani, L. H. & Camaloni, L. (1983). 'Effects of familiarity on peer interaction In the first year of life.' *Early Child Development and Care, 11,* 45–54.

Sundell, K. (1988). 'Day care and children's development. The relations among direct teaching, communicative speech, cognitive performance, and social participation.' *Acta Universitatis Upsaliensu. Studia Psychologica Upsaliensia, 13.* Upsalla University, Sweden.

Tizard, B. (1986). *The care of young children.* Thomas Coram Research Unit Working and Occasional Papers No. 1. Institute of Education, University of London.

Thompson, R. A. (1988). 'The effects of infant day care through the prism of attachment theory: a critical appraisal.' *Early Childhood Research Quarterly, 3,* 273–282.

Weigl, I. & Weber, C. (1990). 'Research in nurseries in the German Democratic Republic.' In E. C. Melhuish and P. Moss (eds.) *Day care for young children: International perspectives.* London: Routledge.

Whitebook, M., Howes, C. & Phillips, D. (1989). *Who Cares? Child Care Teachers and the Quality of Care in America: Executive Summary of the National Child Care Staffing Study.* Oakland: Child Care Employee Project.

Young, G. & Lewis, M. (1979). 'Effects of familiarity and maternal attention on infant peer relations.' *Merrill-Palmer Quarterly, 25,* 105–119.

Day Care in the U.S.A.

Alison Clarke-Stewart

Part One – Kinds and Conditions of day care

Background

Over the past two decades, in the United States, we have seen a dramatic increase in day care for children under five – the result of economic recession, increased participation by women in the labor force, an increase in the number of single parent families, welfare legislation that requires recipients to go to school or get a job, and an increased emphasis on educational programs for younger and younger children. Now, about half of the children under two have mothers who are employed and spend a significant portion of their time with a babysitter, a neighbour, a relative, a paid care provider or in a day care center. For older preschool children the numbers are even higher; about 60 per cent are in day care.

This represents an 80 per cent increase since 1970. Every year the number of young children in some form of day care or early education programme increases markedly. It is estimated that by 1995 at least two-thirds of the mothers of children under five will be in the labor force and at least three-quarters of these children will be in some form of non-parental care.

This is not the result of any government design to lure women to the workplace. Women are flooding the workplace for one reason: money. Because of the decline in real family income since 1970, two-parent families in the US now find it necessary for both parents to work to support the family at a level that used to be achieved by one wage earner alone. Divorced, single, and widowed mothers must work to support themselves and their dependents, because child and spousal support is limited and declining. Even among those mothers who currently are at home, as many as 30 per cent would prefer to work and bring in extra income if day care was available.

In 1970, the White House Conference on Children voted child care the most serious problem facing American families. The same might be said in 1990. For despite some noble attempts to deal with the matter over the past 20 years, the US has not come one step closer to a solution. There is still no national policy on child care and no policy in sight. Experts now talk about the child care 'crisis,' and in the current session of

Congress, legislation to establish some federal aid for child care is at the top of the list of priorities. Right now, Congress is considering a new bill (the A B C Bill or Act for Better Child Care). This Act, supported and actively lobbied for by some 80 organizations, including the American Psychological Association, the American Academy of Pediatrics, and the American Federation of Teachers, would establish an Office of Child Care in the Department of Health and Human Services, and pour $10 – 14 billion over the next 4 years into day care. But even if the Bill does become law, it will be a drop in the bucket of child care need and there will still be no child care system in place to benefit from the funds.

At present, child care is a patchwork quilt, varying from state to state and family to family. It is a patchwork quilt stitched together with a mix of public and private funding, public and private delivery, and a variety of systems for monitoring and regulation.

Forms of day care

There are two major types of day care used by employed mothers in the U S A: home care and centre care. Most families use some kind of home care (see Table 1). Altogether 85 per cent of parents of infants and toddlers (children under 3) and 67 per cent of parents of preschoolers (3 and 4 year olds) use some kind of home care. About one-quarter of the families in which mothers are employed manage to cover child care by juggling the two parents' schedules or by taking the child along to work. Another one-quarter use relatives – aunts, grandmothers, older siblings. Care by relatives is especially common for infants, for black children, for poor children and for children whose mothers have part time jobs.

Table 1

Primary day care arrangements used by employed mothers for their children under 5: U S, 1989

Type of day care	Children under 3 years	Children 3–4 years
Parental	25%	23%
Other relative	27%	21%
Sitter	7%	5%
Day care home	26%	18%
Centre	16%	33%

A few families (about 6 per cent) use a non-related caregiver who comes to or lives in their home – a sitter, a nanny, an au pair, a housekeeper. Again, this form of day care is relatively more common for infants. The last kind of home care is family day care ('childminders'), in which a non-related caregiver cares for a number of children (usually between 5 and 7 children), perhaps including her own, in her home. About one-quarter of the preschool children with employed mothers are in day care homes, but this arrangement is most common arrangement for 1- and 2-year-olds whose mothers are employed full-time.

For 3- and 4-year-olds whose mothers have full-time jobs the most common arrangement is a day care centre; about one-third are in this type of care. In addition to children with employed mothers, many children whose mothers are at home attend day care centres or nursery schools. Currently about half of all 3- and 4-year-olds in the US attend some kind of centre-based preschool programme. For infants and toddlers, only 16 per cent of those whose mothers are employed are in centres (and no non-employed mothers are currently enrolling their 4-month-olds in centres).

Over the past two decades the most significant change in the pattern of day care use has been the increase in the proportion of children using centres. This is true for all ages, from 0 to 4, but most notably for infants; since 1982 alone the proportion of centre day care use for infants has increased from 8 per cent to 20 per cent. Centres are increasing not only in absolute numbers – day care centre capacity has more than doubled in the last decade – but in relative popularity as well. What has decreased though is not the use of day care homes, but the use of non-related babysitters in the child's own home.

Who is responsible for day care?
– the Public Sector

With the dramatic increase in the numbers of employed mothers and the number of children in day care over the past 20 years, particularly in the most public form of day care provided in centres, one might imagine that the government would have been an active participant, or leader, in this social trend. One would be wrong. The increase in the supply of day care is not the result of federal policy but the result of demand by middle-class parents, ignored by Washington. And the crazy patchwork quilt structure of day care provision is not the result of federal planning, but, to use a distinctly American expression, just growed like Topsy. For the last 20 years, the American Government has resisted getting involved in day care. In the 1970s, day care was ignored by the federal government; in the 1980s it was removed from federal auspices.

Back in the 1960s – the good old days

But it was not always so. In the 1960s, when the number of employed mothers first began its rapid ascent, the federal government was actively involved. It funded a variety of programmes, administered by several different federal agencies. There was also involvement in setting standards for the day care programmes that it funded. At first, because the programmes were required to have a state license to receive federal funds,

States began to develop their own licensing standards. But by the late 60s, when it was obvious that there were substantial differences among the states in the standards they were developing, the feds stepped in. In 1968 the Federal Interagency Day Care Requirements were published, establishing requirements for day care centres and day care homes. These F I D C R specified levels of staff training, safety and sanitation, health and nutrition, educational and social services, parent involvement, adult child ratios (1:3 for infants, 1:5 for 2- and 3-year-olds, 1:7 for 4-year-olds), and group sizes (10 for under 3s, 16 for 3s, and 20 for 4-year-olds).

Although compliance with the F I D C R was not mandated, non-compliance was grounds for suspension or termination of any federal funds being received. However, in actuality, even in the good old days, such action was never taken. The F I D C R also stated that facilities receiving federal dollars must be evaluated periodically, but no agent for evaluation was specified. Each federal agency that administered a day care programme was given responsibility for enforcing the F I D C R in that programme. But most agencies did not strictly enforce them because compliance was financially impossible for many programmes and enforcement would have meant a loss of federal funding that would have forced programmes to close.

In order to resolve this situation, the Comprehensive Child Development Act was developed by concerned child development experts, child care advocates, and House and Senate representatives. This proposed legislation, which was accepted by Congress, would have established a national network of day care facilities available to all citizens and adhering to a uniform set of standards. But hopes of a national day care policy and system were shortlived. The Comprehensive Child Development Act was 'nixed' by Nixon in 1971, because he thought it would bring about the demise of the American family.

The not so good 1970s and the really bad 1980s

In the 1970s day care in the U S started to go downhill. In 1975 the ratio requirements in F I D C R were suspended, and in the 1980s, when Reagan took over, things got worse. The Reagan administration made changes in day care as in other social services following the guiding conservative principles of decentralization, deregulation, and privatization. In 1981, Reagan cut direct federal funding for day care services. Federal standards (F I D C R) were eliminated completely. The states became completely responsible for regulating and monitoring day care programmes. State and local communities became the arenas for policy and planning. Incentives were provided for private sector financing and delivery of services. These incentives were primarily tax incentives for businesses and individuals: for example, welfare mothers could deduct money for day care from other earned income; self-supporting families could deduct up to 20–30 per cent of day care costs from their taxable income; employers could establish tax-saving 'salary reduction plans' for employees (discussed further below), and could depreciate their physical facilities if they provided day care. As another encouragement for the private sector, more public subsidy became available for family day care homes.

The only direct federal support for services was food subsidies to day care centers and day care homes for low income children, block grants to states and communities for social services to low income families, and continued funding of Head Start, a pre-school programme for disadvantaged 4-year-olds. Head Start is the only programme with a good record of funding in the 1980s and a good prognosis of funding in the 1990s, but its 1200 centres serve only 16 per cent of the children who are eligible and it does not fill the need for full-time care.

Overall, the results of the federal government's decentralization, deregulation, and privatization were negative. Although, in some states, in the 1980s, funding for day care increased and growth in public school based programmes occurred, most states raised fees, cut back services, reduced their standards (once there was no F I D C R), made the standards apply to fewer institutions (for example, not to church-related or part-time centres), and enforced the standards less stringently and consistently. Discrepancies between states increased.

This led to an increase in the diversity of day care options – a goal of the Reagan administration – but reduction in federal spending curtailed the options of low income families, especially those preferring centre-based care. It also led to a decline in the quality of care available to low income parents. Private day care programmes, which increased in availability as public ones decreased, operate more economically than publicly funded programmes because they have larger classes and pay teachers lower wages – and, as a consequence, they offer lower quality care.

The situation today

Today, most day care in the U S is informal and unregulated. Care in the family's own home or by a relative is completely outside the purview or interest of any government agencies. The only kinds of regulated service are day care centres and day care homes providing care for at least 3 children. Whether day care homes are registered or licensed varies from state to state. Licensing is required or available in about one-half of the states. Thirteen states have voluntary registration. Several states do not require that day care homes be regulated at all (either licensed or monitored), and even in those states that do have such a requirement, the vast majority operate underground; estimates of the proportion of day care homes that are unlicensed range around 90 per cent. Standards also vary; only Massachusetts has the F I D C R recommended ratio of 1:3 for infants; many states have ratios as high as 1:8.

All states regulate centres, but again there is no agreement on standards or on the level of regulation. In most states. regulation consists of an annual inspection to get a licence to operate, with exceptions made for church-run and part-day programmes. But standards vary widely from state to state. In Massachusetts, centre leaders have to be trained in child development and the staff-child ratio for infants is 1:3; in Georgia teachers have to have a high school diploma and the staff-child ratio for infants is 1:7. Staff child ratios for 4-year olds range from 1:5 to 1:20 in different states.

The level of state government involvement also varies from state to state. The most comprehensive involvement and investment is in states like Massachusetts and California. California has the largest day care budget in the U S This includes a mix of funding, covering county day care programmes; resource and referral services; a vendor-voucher program, in which payment for day care for children of poor, single mothers is made directly to the day care provider; and assistance to day care providers through such means as a 'warm' (telephone) line for advice about child health, child behavior problems and a babysitter 'sharing' program. Other states have much less.

The current climate and hopes for future government involvement

But the tide may be turning again. Last year Congress considered over a hundred child care bills, the most promising of which is the A B C Bill. Not only would this bill establish a federal Office of Child Care, but it would provide more tax credits for parents and day care providers, offer services to low income families, provide assistance to providers for getting liability insurance, and set up a committee to draft model standards for states to follow or adapt.

The A B C Bill is an effort to strengthen the federal role in funding day care and assuring quality through regulation. Its primary goal is to help provide day care for low and moderate income families, but it provides incentives for states to improve the quality of all types of care for all families. It also is concerned with promoting adequate administration and co-ordination of child care policies and resources.

The Office of Child Care would be responsible for reviewing state requests for child care funds, for disseminating funds appropriated through the A B C Bill, and for co-ordinating all activities of H H S and other federal agencies relating to child care. It would also collect and publish summaries of state care standards annually. A National Advisory Committee would develop minimum federal standards for centre-based and family day care programmes (including ratios, group sizes, and qualifications of staff). Regulations for ratios and group sizes would initially be based on the current median levels across the states. The minimum standard for caregiver qualification would be at least 15 hours per year of in-service training, and states would be directed to work with institutions of higher learning to develop training for day care personnel. States would also be directed to develop effective licensing procedures so that inspections of facilities and providers could be done in a timely manner. Licensing staff would be directed to make at least one unannounced annual inspection of each centre and to do so for at least 20 per cent of the state's family day care homes.

The A B C Bill passed the Senate in June 1989, but there are still major wrinkles to iron out in the House of Representatives (particularly whether to distribute funds through block grants to States or direct payments to parents and day care facilities and how much money to put into the programme anyway).

In the meantime, if government is not involved in providing day care, who is? For one, schools are.

Schools

Along with the overall increase in day care, there has been a marked growth in supply of pre-school programmes in the last 10 years. All states now provide kindergarten for 5-year-olds and many are going in the direction of providing pre-kindergarten for 4-year-olds. At present these pre-kindergarten programmes are for disadvantaged children only, but eventually they might be available for all children. At the same time, schools have increased the availability of extended-day kindergartens – kindergartens that extend to 1 or 2 in the afternoon. But these kindergarten and pre-K programmes, even if extended to 2 in the afternoon, are not day care, and do not, alone, meet the needs of employed parents.

It has recently been suggested, however, that schools could provide the solution to the day care crisis. So called 'new schools' would offer day care in school buildings, administered through the school system, with satellite networks of all the day care homes in the neighborhood, and accompanied by parent education outreach programmes. These school-based day care centres would be staffed by personnel with degrees in early childhood education or child development, not by elementary school teachers. They would offer a balance of academic and non-academic activities, not just be an extension of the elementary school curriculum downward.

This idea of day care in the school has several justifications: (1) schools are the most reliable, permanent, and stable institution in society, not contingent on year to year funding; (2) schools could offer equal access to child care for all children who need it because they are open to all children; (3) schools have as their goal the optimal development of children, not the goal of allowing parents to work or of helping the needy; (4) teachers are better paid than day care workers today and having day care in the schools could lead to the upgrading of these workers' salaries. Bills proposing such demonstration schools of the 21st century are before Congress this session, and some states already have them.

Of course there are concerns about tying day care to the schools: in particular, concerns about the academization of day care (because kindergarten has become academic), and concerns that removing pre-schoolers from home day care will make that form of day care unaffordable for infants and toddlers (because a caregiver can care for fewer infants and toddlers than pre-schoolers). But most people conclude that if the U S is to have an adequate system of day care, schools will have to play a large part. Schools are the only institution with the societal mission and potential capacity to make universal provision. But that is in the future.

The private sector

For now, the bulk of day care is sponsored and funded not by the public sector, including schools, but by the private sector: by employers, charitable organizations, entrepreneurs, and parents. This was the solution favoured by the Reagan administration: privatization. Employers and charitable agencies were to take up the slack when the government abdicated and respond to the needs of employed parents. Unfortunately, this solution has simply not worked.

Employers

Despite inspirational breakfast meetings, Federal Government tax and depreciation incentives, and the example set by state governments who set up model day care facilities for their own employees, only 3500 out of 6 million American employers offer child care assistance of any kind (6/100 of 1 per cent). Employers do not need to try to recruit women employees (women are knocking down their doors), and any effort on their part is because they are under pressure from government, media, or child care advocates. Consequently, when employers do make a contribution to day care, it is usually through referral and information – the least costly possible contribution. Sometimes they offer salary reduction plans (where employers set aside a sum of non-taxable income from employees earnings, for day care costs). But neither of these contributions increases the supply of day care. Provision of actual on-site day care is the least likely contribution for an employer to make.

In a representative survey of 600 adults in U S households with incomes over $25,000 in 1987, the overwhelming majority wanted employers to be more involved in day care: 58 per cent wanted day care subsidies, 70 per cent wanted on-site day care, 80 per cent wanted employers to offer day care referrals, and 84 per cent wanted employers to offer flexible work hours so they could make better day care arrangements. Of these adults, only 4 per cent had day care subsidized by their employer, 5 per cent had on-site day care, 9 per cent were given help with day care referrals, and 19 per cent had flexible hours at work; 39 per cent of the adults surveyed would consider changing jobs if they knew of a company that offered on-site day care.

But employees (and employers) who actually have on-site care are disillusioned. Most employees do not like it and most employers find it too expensive to establish, too risky to operate, too complicated to administer, and too likely to be underused. Employers just do not want to get into day care and they are not.

Charities

Nor are charitable organizations, the second element in the private sector, taking up the gauntlet. Historically in the US the largest suppliers of day care have been private, non-profit providers. Over last 20 years, however, there has been a decline in the proportion of non-profit day care facilities and increase in for-profit facilities. Charitable organizations do not have the money or the manpower (womanpower) to provide the day care the country needs.

The child care industry

To whom then does the provision of day care fall? To the for-profit day care providers. Who are they? Everyone from the auntie down the street to Gerber Baby Foods; from women who are at home with their own children and need some extra income to ambitious new graduates of business schools and psychology departments; from specially trained nannies to illegal immigrants who do not speak English but will do housework as well as care for children.

Child care in America is business – big business. Family day care homes are the most numerous, cheapest, and most elastic of the for-profit day care arrangements. There is no need for construction of a facility, no need to set up a complex administrative structure. Day care homes offer a range of opportunities for the provider, from the most informal and casual taking-in of a few kids on the side to a thoroughly professional effort in a registered, licensed home that may even be part of a network of day care homes affiliated with a school, university, or day care centre. Most day care homes tend to be informal, unprofessional, and shortlived. They offer experiences for the child ranging from concerned and competent care by an involved and happy care provider to neglectful or even abusive care by a depressed and isolated woman who believes she has no marketable skills but needs the money and so takes in babies.

More expensive to set up but also growing in popularity as a business are for-profit centres. Currently about half of the day care centres in the US operate for profit; 2,000 of these are in day care chains (like Kindercare, which now has 1,200 centres in over 40 states and brings in an income of over $200 million annually), but most are single centre, 'mom and pop' operations. Most of these proprietary centers offer full-day care. This care may be excellent, educational, individualized, and stimulating – or it may consist of custodial care in a baby warehouse. The level of quality in the centre is very much linked to the state or county requirements for licensing. Proprietary day care centres do not have ratios and group sizes better than the government requires, because to make a profit requires the largest possible number of children for each adult salary.

From all these possibilities – publicly subsidized and privately supported day care centres and day care homes, good and bad – it is up to parents in the free market to put together a day care arrangement, to find an acceptable day care facility, to get their child into it, to monitor it, pay for it, worry about it, to pick out or create their own patch in the patchwork quilt, drawing on whatever resources they have from Grandma Jane to connections at the neighborhood nursery school. For American families finding day care is catch as catch can. Day care is as necessary for most American families as an automobile and a refrigerator, but infinitely harder to find and more expensive to buy.

Parents must pay the bulk of day care fees for their children from their incomes, assisted only by the child care tax credit. For families with children, day care is their fourth largest expenditure (after food, housing, taxes). Affluent families (making over $45,000 a year) manage to swing this, paying on an average about $60 a week for day care, which works out at just 4 per cent of their income. But poor families, making under $15,000 a year, pay an average of $33 a week or 20 per cent of their income.

Access and use

So what do parents do? Most of them, as I pointed out earlier, at first, use home care. Although the proportion of parents using day care centres has increased over the last 20 years, home care still is the most common day care for under threes (60 per cent). One reason that parents choose home care might be that they think it is better for very young children because it is more like being with mother. But parents change home care arrangements every year, on average – because they are dissatisfied, or because they think the child needs a different kind of experience, or because the home care provider quits; and parents say they would prefer to move their children into centres if slots were available.

So parents probably are not using home day care just because they prefer that form of care. They are using home day care because it is what is available and affordable. For the under threes, welfare mothers use relative care, which tends to be free or cheap. Middle income mothers use unregulated day care homes, which are moderately inexpensive. Only high income mothers use the more expensive in-home sitters or care in sponsored day care homes.

For 3- and 4-year-olds, most parents, but especially those who are more highly educated and have higher incomes, use centres, because centres are more available for 3- and 4-year-olds and because parents think that centre care is better for children by this age. Parents like centres because of their convenience, because they offer the child learning experiences, and because those experiences change as the child gets older. Parents using centres do not change to day care homes.

But although all parents prefer and use day care centres for their 3- and 4-year-olds, they do not all have equal success in finding good quality centres. The U.S. has a three-tiered system of centre-based care: (1) affluent families purchase places in high quality expensive private centres; (2) low income families have access to high quality centres subsidized by the state; (3) but the families in the middle, the working class and lower-middle class, must settle for marginal or inadequate centres.

How bad is the day care that parents can purchase?

In the recently completed National Child Care Staffing Study, a survey of 227 day care centres in 5 cities, the quality of care in the majority of centres was rated as barely adequate. Staff turnover in American day care centres now averages 41 per cent per year, while for day care home providers it is 59 per cent. These turnover rates have tripled in last 10 years. The major reason? low wages. For despite the fact that workers in day care centres are more highly educated than the average American worker – in the National Staffing Study, for example, 65 per cent of teacher and 56 per cent of assistant teachers had completed course work in early childhood or child development at a high school, vocational school, college or graduate school – they are abysmally underpaid. Sixty percent earn less than $5/hour; the average annual wage of a day care teacher is just over $9,000 (the 1988 poverty threshold for a family of 3), while 90 per cent of day care home providers earn less than poverty level wages.

Child care workers have never been well paid, but their wages have decreased over 20 per cent in the last decade. They are now the second most underpaid workers in the US, next to the clergy, according to the National Committee on Pay Equity. They earn less than half what comparably educated women in other professions earn, less than one-third as much as comparably educated men. And of course they do not have health insurance or retirement plans.

So the day care situation in America, as a result of the non-involvement of either government or industry, is apparently not only patchy but of poor and declining quality. Why is it so bad? The situation reflects the national ambivalence about day care. We have the knowledge to provide quality services in the US – what is lacking is the will and the way to do so. According to some experts, when 80 per cent of the women in the country are employed, the cost of day care will be covered by the property tax, and, in the meantime, it could be covered by fees on a sliding scale and government subsidies. But providing universal day care is not part of the American agenda; it is not consistent with American values and ideologies which stress the importance of exclusive maternal care for children, the self reliance of families, the need for family privacy, the desire for individual options and choices, and the virtue of the free market system.

Day care has a bad reputation in America. It has filled multiple roles throughout US history, but basically it has always been something for poor, inadequate families. In the beginning there were the day nurseries for children of poor immigrant, single mothers; then there was day care as part of the War on Poverty, a vehicle for the education of disadvantaged children or their parents. Most recently it has become a means of allowing welfare mothers to get out and get jobs. Day care has never been viewed as a right of children or a need of employed parents.

Lessons

Of course there are major differences between the United States and Great Britain – in history, economics, even values. Britain has national health, maternity leave and part-time employment for women; America does not. But Britain also has experienced Margaret Thatcher and privatization, and its people share some of the values regarding maternal care and family privacy that have kept the US from a national child care policy. Perhaps there are lessons that might be learned from the American experience. Lessons like the following:

- mothers are going to go out to work;
- children are going to need day care;
- for that care parents prefer centers;
- and at least in the short run, decentralization, deregulation, and privatization are likely to lead to a decline in day care organization and quality especially for poor families.

Part Two – Quality and Consequences

A question that concerns us all, given this gloomy picture of day care provision, is just what effects day care as compared with traditional care by parents at home has on children's development. It has been suggested by experts in and out of the field of child development, as recently as last week, that day care is bad for children, especially for babies. And judging by the bleak statistics on day care in America, this would not be surprising. But for the most part, these experts have only been guessing about the effects of day care in line with their beliefs about what is best for mothers and for children; because, until quite recently, systematic, empirical data about day care effects were lacking.

Actual studies of day care did not begin until the 1970s. Since that time, a sizable number of studies have been undertaken, and now we are beginning to get some answers. Those answers are not simple, however, and they may be getting out of date if the day care system deteriorates further.

In presenting the results of the studies, I will make the answers as simple as possible. There are many discrepancies and confusions in the findings that I do not have the time (or inclination) to go into. But even drawing the simplest possible picture of the results leaves room for interpretation.

Day care for two to four year olds

To begin with, there is the question of whether day care is good for children's mental or intellectual development. Here, the answer is perhaps clearest. There is a substantial body of research that suggests that within the limits of the day care programmes that have been studied – and clearly this does not include the most inadequate day care – day care is not harmful to children, and may even help their development.

In the two dozen or so studies in the U S comparing the development of children who attended day care centers, nursery schools, or early childhood programs in the pre-school years (ages 2 to 4 years) with the development of children from comparable family backgrounds who did not, only one that I know of showed that children in day care programmes do more poorly in overall intellectual development than children at home. That was a study of poor day care, in which adult:child ratios for 2- and 3-year olds averaged 1 adult to 20 children. The other studies, presumably of better services, all showed that children in day care programmes do at least as well – and sometimes better – on tests of mental or intellectual development. To be more specific, on the average across these studies, children in day care:

- scored higher on I Q tests (tests which tap a variety of different skills, from knowing the definitions of words, to being able to put pictures together to make a coherent and logical story and being able to copy the patterns that the examiner makes with different coloured blocks);

- were more advanced in their eye-hand co-ordination (that is, they could do activities like drawing, building with blocks, cutting and pasting, at younger ages); were more creative in the ways in which they explored and played with materials (they did not just use toys and other materials in standard, stereotyped ways – trucks go 'vroom, vroom' – but came up with original uses – trucks can be used for doing laundry in);

- knew more about the physical world – about animals, and plants and seasons;

- had more of the beginning arithmetic skills like counting and measuring before they went to school;

- could remember and recite back information more accurately, including their names and addresses;

- and were able to use and understand more advanced language – their vocabularies were larger, and they could follow more complicated directions, put words together into longer sentences.

In a study of 2 to 4 year old children that I did, for instance, children who were in nursery school and day care centre programmes were, on the average, 6 to 9 months ahead of children cared for at home by their mothers or babysitters or in day care homes on tests of these kinds of intellectual competence.

This advanced development, the research suggests, reflects a temporary gain in these children's development during the pre-school years. It is a speeding up in the rate of their early acquisition of these kinds of mental abilities, these kinds of competent behavior; it is not a permanent enhancement of their abilities. The gains last only as long as the children are in the day care programme. By the time they have gone through first grade, children who did not have experience in a pre-school programme generally have caught up with those who did. The gains are also not cumulative; they are not linked to the length of time children are in the day care programme or to the age at which they started. They show up by the time the children have been in day care for a year, then level off and do not get bigger after that.

Gains are most evident in the school-related behaviors and abilities described above. They do not appear in all aspects of development (e.g., emotional adjustment, relations with parents, empathy and social sensitivity). However, pre-school children who attend day care programmes, were also likely to be:

- more self-confident, outgoing, assertive, and self-sufficient;

- more comfortable in new situations, less timid and fearful;

- more helpful and co-operative;

- more verbally expressive (they didn't just talk better, they talked more);

- they knew more about social rules and norms (for example, that it is worse to hit another kid than not to be quiet when the teacher is talking, or what the stereotypes are of the kinds of toys that boys and girls should play with);

- but despite their knowledge of what boys and girls 'should' play with, in their own play they were less likely to play in gender role stereotyped ways;

- and finally, they were better liked by adults who met them.

These differences did not appear in all studies of all centres for all children, but when differences did appear, they were in this direction.

So, considering all this research, it looks like day care – at least the day care that has been studied – is basically good or at least OK for children.

But wait. That was the good news. Now for the bad news. The research has also shown that children in day care, in addition to having these good qualities, were also generally (on the average, and in America, of course):

- less polite (less likely to say please and thank you);

- less agreeable (less likely to say 'Yes, mother, I'll do it.');

- less compliant with their mother's or caregiver's demands and requests (more likely to say 'No, I won't do it');

- louder and more boisterous (shouting 'No, I won't do it' as they run around the room);

- more irritable ('I want my supper now') and more rebellious ('I won't go to bed.' I won't brush my teeth.' 'You're not the boss of me.');

- more likely to use bad language (using naughty words, not poorly constructed sentences – 'I won't do it, dammit!);

- and in the words of one immortal headline they were 'thirteen times more aggressive' than children who were not in, or who had not been in, day care (they were more likely to punch and kick other children and call them dirty names).

These differences in social behavior appeared in tests and in natural observations, in the day care centre and on the playground, with adults and with other children, with strangers and with parents; they appeared for both boys and girls, and for children from both model and mediocre day care programmes. They were more marked for children from lower income families, but they also appeared for middle class kids.

The problem, obviously, is how to interpret these differences. Are day care children more socially competent or less? They are helpful but also demanding, co-operative but also bossy, friendly but also aggressive, outgoing but also rude. As one person pointed out, this sounds like a personality description of an effective company president. My own interpretation is that in the pre-school years day care children as a group are developmentally advanced in the social realm, just as they are in the intellectual realm, which is why they are more knowledgeable, self-sufficient, and able to co-operate; but they are also more determined to get their own way and they do not always have the social skills to achieve this smoothly, which is why they are also more aggressive, irritable, and non-compliant.

But these are general statements about all children in all day care centre or nursery school programmes compared with all children at home. These findings are based on differences between groups of children, not individuals. They are based on a sample of centres of relatively high quality. Do all day care programmes by their very nature have these effects, or are some programmes better than others at enhancing children's intelligence or worse than others for promoting children's aggressiveness? What is it about day care programmes that enhances children's intellectual development or increases their aggressiveness?

Consistent with common sense and casual observation, researchers have discovered that there are differences in children's development related to the kinds of day care programmes they are in. Distilling the results from all the studies linking children's development to different kinds of day care programmes, I have identified four different aspects of day care programmes that seem to be particularly related to children's behavior and development – the physical environment, the caregiver's behavior, the curriculum, and the number of children.

The physical environment	Surprisingly, perhaps, the results of studies of children in day care centres show that children's intellectual and social development is not related to the number of toys available or to the amount of physical space available, unless it is extremely crowded (which does have negative effects). What matters more is the organization of the space and the quality of the materials available. Children, as any tidy and sensitive grandmother might have predicted, do better in centres that are neat, clean, safe, and orderly, that are organized into interest areas and oriented toward children's activities. They do better in centres with toys and materials that are varied and educational. Children are more likely to do constructive, mentally challenging things with building materials, to have interesting and mature conversations in play using dramatic props, to co-operate with peers in social games like checkers and pick-up sticks. While having a variety of materials adds to the range of children's educational experiences.

So the general conclusion to draw from the research on the physical environment is that it is not quantity but quality that matters most. Simply adding more balls or games or space does not necessarily improve the programme or enhance children's development, if the center already has some balls and some games and enough space. What is more, simply adding materials to pre-school classrooms or having more varied materials does not lead to cognitive gains, except in combination with teachers' behavior. Which brings us to the second important aspect of the day care program.

Caregivers' behaviour	Children are more likely to develop social and intellectual skills if the caregivers in their day care centres are:

- responsive (they answer the children's questions, respond to their requests);
- positive (giving praise, smiles, making life in the day care centre enjoyable);
- accepting (following the children's suggestions as well as listening to them, praising the child who does it wrong as well as the one who does it right);
- informative in their interactions with the children (giving reasons, explanations, lessons).

Children's development is advanced if their teachers:

- read to them;

- and offer them choices and give them gentle suggestions; rather than:

- simply hugging and holding them;

- helping them (unless the child asks for help);

- and directing, controlling, restricting, and punishing them.

These kinds of teacher behavior have been associated with poorer development, rather than advanced development, in day care children. In my study, for instance, caregivers who initiated more physical contact, physical help and physical control with the children they were in charge of, had children who did more poorly in the asssessments we made of their social and mental competence. Children in this and other studies do best when interactions with the caregiver are stimulating, educational and respectful, not custodial or demeaning.

If teachers are very busy and there are many children demanding their attention, it seems to make a difference just how much one-to-one conversation the teachers manage to have with the children. But if conversation is relatively frequent, once again it is the quality of the one-to-one conversation (its positive tone, responsive and accepting nature, informative content) that seems to be more important than the sheer amount. Again, we see that once a floor of quantity has been achieved, it is quality of care that matters.

Researchers of course have also asked how these positive kinds of behavior – responsive, accepting, positive and informative – are associated with the caregiver's background. Their studies show that caregivers who are most likely to behave in these positive ways are those with more experience as child care professionals, those who have been in the day care programme longer, and those who have higher levels of training in children development. On all these dimensions, however, the relation appears to be a curvilinear one; that is, past a certain point, having more experience or more stability or more training is not advantageous.

Teachers who have more professional experience are likely to be more responsive, accepting, positive, and so on, than teachers with less experience, but only up to about 10 years or so of experience. Teachers with more than 15 years experience in the field have been observed in several studies of day care to provide less stimulating and educational interaction than caregivers with less experience. There are several possible explanations for this finding: the most likely are burnout (teachers just get worn down after years of challenging and demanding working conditions, constant giving of themselves, for meagre economic rewards); generational or age effects (the younger generation of teachers may be more positive than the older generation); or selective attrition (the better teachers have become administrators or politicians). We need further research to sort out these possibilities.

Stability of the caregiver in a particular day care setting, similarly, is positively related to the quality of care, while conversely staff turnover is clearly negatively related; the more staff changes the worse for the programme. In the National Child Care Staffing Study, centres rated higher on overall quality, centres in which children spent less time in aimless wandering and scored higher on a test of intelligence, had lower turnover. Staff stability is an important aspect of day care quality, not only because it is good for children to form relationships with their daily caregivers and vice versa, but also, I suspect, because such stability indicates that the centre offers good working conditions, adequate wages, and high morale.

Staying in one day care centre for three or four years is therefore a positive sign, and within this period staying longer is better. But the relationship between stability and quality is curvilinear; beyond three or four years, staying longer does not improve the quality of care the caregiver provides. What is important is offering adequate wages and benefits to entice teachers to stay for more than a year. In the National Staffing Study, turnover was related to low wages and the number one suggestion for how to improve quality, made by 90 per cent of the teachers sampled, was to pay better salaries for child care work.

In the National Staffing Study, too, higher quality centres had better educated and trained teachers. This association between training and quality of care has appeared in many earlier studies and caregiver training is now generally considered to be a sine qua non of quality care. But, here again, the picture is not so simple. Although having no training in child development is clearly worse than having some, more training is not a guarantee of better care; taking 10 courses is not necessarily better than taking 6. It depends on the content, quality and variety of the courses. As it is, there is some suggestion that when teachers have taken more training in child development (at least in the courses that are available or that are most likely to be taken by day care workers in America) they develop an academic orientation, which translates in the day care classroom into an emphasis on school activities (reading, counting, lesson, learning) to the exclusion of activities to promote children's social or emotional development. Formal training in child development is indeed good background for providing a day care environment that promotes children's intellectual development, but it is not necessarily so good for children's social development. In my study, for example, the caregivers who had had more formal training in child development had children who were advanced intellectually but were significantly less competent in interactions with unfamiliar peers.

Curriculum

The same kind of findings appear when researchers examine the significance of the day care programme's curriculum – the third important component of day care. Having some kind of a curriculum – some lessons, some structure, some organized and supervised activities – clearly is better than having none. But having too much structure, too much regimentation is bad. Children in day care need to express their needs and interests and the day's activities cannot all be planned by the teacher. Children benefit from the opportunity and encouragement to explore and play and learn on their own. On the other hand, 32 children who spend their time in day care just playing with other children and have no educational activities or teacher direction do not make the gains in intellectual or social development that have been observed in other children.

As far as the type of curriculum goes – Montessori, Piagetian, Distar, etc. – it seems that this is not critical for the children's intellectual development; there are apparently many curricula available and in use today that promote the acquisition of children's intellectual knowledge. But it may matter more to children's social and motivational development. Children who are most likely to be co-operative, self-confident, assertive, and aggressive have teachers who, directly and indirectly, are most likely to encourage the children's self direction and independence, co-operation and knowledge, self expression and social interaction, intellectual development and academic skills – but who do not focus on teaching the children social skills. Those day care children who were observed to interact more aggressively with other children (including those who were 13 times more aggressive, for example) came from model, university-based programs, which were particularly focused on promoting the children's intellectual development. Children who have developed social skills in day care or early childhood education programs, children who have learned non-aggressive strategies for solving social problems (like how to get the wheel barrow they want for instance), do not pick them up incidentally by hanging around in a benign and permissive environment with other children, even if they are saying their abc's or building with blocks together. These social skills come only from day care programmes in which special efforts were made to teach them. In the most satisfactory day care, it appears, children are offered a balanced menu of social and intellectual lessons.

Number of children

Finally, the last important dimension of day care that I have picked out to mention is the number of children who are in the programme or in the class. Repeating the themes of quality versus quantity and how you can have too much of a good thing, the research on this dimension suggests that although the opportunity to interact with other children in day care is good – because other children offer advanced models of behavior, direct tutoring, and challenging play – simply having more and more interaction with other children typically is not so good. When children spend more of their time in the day care centre just watching, playing around with, fighting, and imitating other children (especially younger children), they tend to be less competent socially and intellectually.

Often the reason children spend their time in day care just hanging around with the other kids is that the group is large (for 3–4 year olds, larger than 20) or that the ratio of adults to children is low (lower than 1:10). We are all well aware of the importance of group or class size and adult:child ratio as indexes and indeed causes of better or worse day care. But again, what recent research suggests is that the relation is not a simple one. It seems that a poor adult:child ratio may be more damaging than a high adult child ratio is beneficial. That is, in a class of 4 year olds, the difference between an adult:child ratio of 1:10 and an adult:child ratio of 1:14 is probably more significant – that is, makes more difference to the quality of the child's experience and the child's development – than the difference between an adult:child ratio of 1:10 and an adult:child ratio of 1:6.

The importance of the adult:child ratio also depends on the children's ages. Adult:child ratio and class size seem to be more important for 2-year-olds than they do for 4-year-olds. The younger the child the more important it is for him or her to get adequate attention from an adult and not to get overwhelmed by a bunch of rowdy toddlers or to get lost in a crowd of nameless (grubby) faces.

In sum then, these four aspects of day care – the physical setting, the caregiver's behavior, the curriculum, and the number of children – are linked to children's behavior and development in ways that are clear and sensible, but not simple. One way in which the relation is not simple is that on these dimensions, more is not necessarily better – whether it be more training, more experience, or more time in the center for the caregiver; more toys or more space; more structure or more academic activities; more direction or more physical contact from the caregiver; more other children to play with or more time to play with them. Another way in which the relation is not simple is that these dimensions, quality seems to matter more than quantity. Beyond the minimal acceptable standards of quantity, it is the quality of the programme that matters –

the organization of the physical space, the responsiveness of the caregivers' behavior, the content of the curriculum and the type of interactions with peers; and not the quantity of the programme – more space, more toys, more interaction with the caregiver or other children, more lessons on the A B C's. Finally, such high quality day care is more likely in centres that are non-profit, especially those that are government subsidized, and in which there is a larger expenditure for each child.

Type of day care

So far, I have been talking about quality in centre day care – because most research is about centres. But given the current day care scene, it is also important to ask whether home day care has the same effects and whether these same indices of quality predict child development outcomes in home day care as well as in centres. There is a little research that speaks to these questions. In day care homes, of course, unlike centres, quality is not usually defined by presence of a curriculum; but the other three dimensions I identified as important in centres do appear to be linked to good care in homes as well. Children do better when the physical environment in the day care home is organized to encourage their activities; when the home care provider has a professional attitude and some training or education; and when there is a moderate number' of children (more than 2, fewer than 10).

As to which type of care is better, centre or home, most people in the field think that either can offer excellent care. But in my study and others, children's development and observed experiences with a sitter or in a day care home were not different from those of children at home with their own mothers. They did not exhibit the advanced competence of the children in day care centres and nursery schools. This may be because in the real world of day care in America, or at least in the centres and homes that have been the targets of study, centres offer, on the average, care and stimulation of higher quality than do homes.

Differences are less when the day care homes are of high quality. For example, in one study, although the competence of children in unregulated day care homes was inferior to that of children in centres, the competence of children in regulated homes was equivalent. More telling, in another study, when care in day care homes was enriched by the experimental addition of a structured educational curriculum, the intellectual competence of the children was observed to improve to the level of children in day care centres. This suggests that although typical practice in centres is often more educational than typical practice in homes, this is probably not a necessary difference between the two environments.

Day care for infants

I have deliberately limited this discussion so far to the research on the effects of day care on children over 2. What about infants who are placed in day care in the first year of life. In the last couple of years in the US, there has been a very heated and noisy debate about whether day care is bad for babies, whether it places them at risk far developing emotional insecurity and causes them to become socially maladjusted.

The major source of the debate is the research assessing infants' relationships with their mothers. The infant-mother relationship is, of course, central in the infant's psychological development. It is also vulnerable, when infants are separated from their mothers for 8 to 10 hours a day. Although research consistently has shown that infants of employed mothers do form relationships with their mothers and prefer their mothers to their substitute caregivers, the question is whether the quality of their relationships is as good, as emotionally secure, as the relationships of infants who are being raised exclusively at home.

As a first step in answering this question, one can look at data from all studies of infants in day care that have included the current standard assessment of children's relationships with their mother. Combining the 16 studies that have used this assessment, it turns out that the infants who are in day care full-time compared with infants who are in day care part-time or not at all are indeed more likely to be classified as having an insecure relationship with their mothers. But the problem is how to interpret this difference. Does the standard assessment that was used really reflect emotional insecurity in these children? And if it does, is the difference large enough that we need to be concerned about it? It is because the difference is open to interpretation that controversy about infant day care is so heated.

To appreciate the problem, you must first consider the assessment on which the judgement that these babies have insecure relationships with their mothers is based. The standard assessment of infants' relationships with their mothers ('the strange situation') involves the following scenario: the infant plays with toys in an unfamiliar room; he is left by his mother alone in the room with an unfamiliar woman; he plays with and is comforted by that woman in his mother's absence; and his mother returns and picks him up. The child's relationship is assessed by observing how he or she responds at this final step when the mother returns to the room. If the child goes to or greets the mother, this is a sign of a secure relationship. If he avoids or ignores her, this is the sign of an insecure relationship.

The problem with this assessment is that this scenario sounds suspiciously like the kind of experience that infants in day care go through regularly. Could it be that infants who have had this kind of experience repeatedly are less likely therefore to seek physical closeness with their mothers – which is the basis for saying their relationship with their mother is insecure. When other methods of assessing infants' relationships with their mothers are used, it turns out that the differences are not as marked. What is more, one must question whether even if babies did have less secure relationships with their mothers, this would mean they were emotionally disturbed. On other measures of emotional adjustment, children who were in day care as infants have been observed to do as well as children who were not, suggesting that day care infants are not more emotionally disturbed overall.

Even if the observed difference in these infants' relationships with their mothers did indicate a degree of emotional insecurity, is the difference big enough that we should be concerned about it? It is the difference between 36 per cent (for children admitted to full-time day care under 12 months) and 29 per cent (for other children). This is a difference that turns out to be within the normal range when one looks at research from around the world. Moreover, the difference is found only in infants from low risk, middle class families; for infants from high risk families, those who are in day care are actually more likely to have secure relationships with their mothers. And it is a difference whose meaning is open to interpretation. The significance of the difference I think lies not in demonstrating that day care is harmful to infants, but in alerting us to possible problems that day care may create for infants.

Another problem that research alerts us to is in the intellectual domain. Recent evidence from the National Longitudinal Study of Youth suggests that boys from high income families in full-time infant care may be at risk for lower intellectual development. There were no negative effects for girls or for children from low income families.

We need to be cautious as we try out different forms and programmes of day care for infants and as we evaluate the effects of these forms and programmes of day care on infants. We need to put our effort into trying to discover under what circumstances infants in day care are likely to suffer. It would not be surprising to discover that some day care is good and some is bad for babies, just as for older children. Perhaps for infants also a certain amount of day care is good and too much day care is bad. Perhaps day care is good for some infants but bad for others. We need to identify the conditions in day care for infants that in combination with the infant's home circumstances and individual constitution are likely to lead to negative – or positive – outcomes, conditions like the kind of training and personal qualities that prepare a person to be a good caregiver, or the maximum number of infants that a caregiver can adequately care for at one time (for while it is clear that no adult regardless of training can provide adequate care and stimulation for 8 infants, let alone evacuate them in an emergency, it is not clear whether the minimum acceptable ratio is 1:5 or 1:4 or 1:3 – or 3:1).

Lessons

What lessons are to be drawn from the research American developmental psychologists have done on the effects of child care and the predictors of high quality?

There are at least four:

(1) Day care is potentially beneficial to pre-school children's development – if it is high quality;

(2) High quality is based on:

- a well organized and stimulating physical environment;

- a responsive and trained caregiver;

- a balanced curriculum;

- and relatively small classes.

(3) Because of the finding that the relation between these dimensions of quality and child development outcomes is curvilinear, it is probably more important at least in the short-run to put our efforts into ensuring that all day care programmes meet minimal acceptable standards (for group/class size, ratio, caregiver training) than to trying to improve the quality of already adequate care;

(4) We are on shakier ground in designing optimal or adequate care for the under twos and should proceed with caution as we provide and study day care for infants over the next decade.

References

This chapter draws on a wide range of American research.

This work is discussed further in the following references:

Clarke-Stewart, K. A. (1989). 'Infant day care: Maligned or malignant'. *American Psychologist 44*, 266–273.

Clarke-Stewart, A. (1982). *Day care*. London: Fontana.

Howes, C. (1990). 'Caregiving environments and their consequences for children: The experience in the United States'. In E. C. Melhuish & P. Moss (Eds.) *Day care for young children: International perspectives*. London: Routledge.

Kahn, A. J., & Kamerman, S. B. (1987). *Child care: Facing the hard choices*. Dover, MA: Auburn House.

Phillips, D. A. (Ed.) (1987). *Quality in child care: What does research tell us?* Washington: National Association for the Education of Young Children.

Phillips, D. A. (1990). 'Day care for young children in the United States'. In E. C. Melhuish & P. Moss (eds.) *Day care for young children: International perspectives*. London: Routledge.

Scarr, S., Phillips, D. & McCartney, K. (1990). 'Facts, fantasies and the future of child care in the United States'. *Psychological Science, 1,* 26–35.

A special issue of *Early Childhood Research Quarterly* contains the following articles on the 'Belsky debate':

Belsky, J. (1988). 'The "effects" of infant day care reconsidered'. *Early Childhood Research Quarterly, 3,* 235–272.

Clarke-Stewart, A. (1988). 'The "effects" of infant day care reconsidered: risks for parents, children, and researchers'. *Early Childhood Research Quarterly, 3,* 293–318.

Richters, J., & Zahn-Waxler, C. (1988). 'The infant day care controversy: current status and future directions'. *Early Childhood Research Quarterly, 3,* 319–336.

Thompson, R.A. (1988). 'The effects of infant day care through the prism of attachment theory: a critical appraisal'. *Early Childhood Research Quarterly, 3,* 273–282.

Day Care in Sweden

Philip Hwang

Part One – Day Care Policy and Provision

Introduction

What are Swedes like? Recently, this question received a lot of attention in the Swedish media. The reason for this was an article in the *Daily Mail* by an English journalist, Geoffrey Levy. He described Swedes as lazy, sick and totally unable to enjoy anything nice in life. In addition, Swedish cars are. wrecks, Swedes dress sloppily and if you do not want to work you do not need to – but you are still fully paid. Finally, he described family policy in Sweden: 'just imagine a country where mothers as well as fathers can stay at home 12 months, with almost full pay after a baby is born, or a country where the state pays almost 6,000 pounds for every child that goes to a day care centre – this would be totally impossible in Britain'.

How did the Swedish public react to Geoffrey Levy's article? Surprisingly, most people agreed with his description of the Swedes. Yes, we are lazy, too many people are sick and we are unable to enjoy the good things in life. There was only one issue where most people disagreed with Geoffrey Levy. Very few were negative about family policy in Sweden. On the contrary, most people took parental leave, the possibility of staying at home with a sick child and publicly-funded day care for granted.

In this first part of the paper, I will describe family policy in Sweden, and in particular how the society supports and provides care for children under school age (which in Sweden starts at 7). This includes different forms of public day care, but also a parental leave programme. The second part of the paper examines the research evidence on the impact of public day care on children's development.

Before starting, just a brief introduction to Sweden. Family patterns have changed dramatically in Sweden during the past few decades. Changes in marriage and increasing numbers of divorces have resulted in new kinds of families being formed. A larger proportion of the adult population play a parental role. The period they play this role, however, is probably shorter than it was for past generations of Swedes due to such factors as the smaller number of children and the increased number of single parent families. In addition, there is a tendency for men and women to become parents at a later age than in previous generations, due partly to spending a longer time in education.

If we look at this picture of family structure from the point of view of the child, we find that most children in Sweden live in families with two cohabiting parents. However 15 per cent live in single-parent families, usually with the mother.

The proportion of mothers in paid work has risen dramatically in the last two decades. In 1964, less than a third of all employed women had children; by 1980, this figure had risen to almost half. The increase has been particularly rapid among women with pre-school children, where the proportion working outside the home more than doubled during the 1960s and 1970s. By 1989, almost 90 per cent of women with preschool children were gainfully employed (including those on parental leave). While in the past there was one wage earner per family, the most common pattern in today's two parent family is that both parents are gainfully employed, the father full-time and the mother part-time: (though it should be noted that mothers with part-time jobs in Sweden work longer hours than mothers with part-time jobs in the UK; in 1988 in Sweden, employed women with a child aged 1–3 averaged 28 hours paid work per week and women with a child aged 4–6 averaged 31 hours, while average hours of paid work for men with children aged 1–3 and 4–6 were 42 and 43 respectively).

A final observation concerns the birth rate. In recent years, this has been increasing markedly after reaching a low point of 1.6 in the early 1980s. Sweden now has the second highest birth rate in Western Europe; the total period fertility rate of 2.06 has nearly reached the level at which the population is again replacing itself, and is not far behind the Republic of Ireland which still has the highest level of fertility in Europe.

The Parental Leave Programme

The parental leave programme developed in the 1970s. Until then, Sweden had provision for maternity leave which had been extended on several occasions since it was first introduced in 1931. In 1974, however, Sweden introduced a system of parental leave which in effect replaced post-natal maternity leave and allowed either parent to stay home from work for 6 months after the birth of a child, or to divide this time as they chose. This programme developed in response to three major concerns: (1) worry about a low birth rate;(2) the need to encourage women's employment (as the programme gives fathers the opportunity to stay at home and the mother to go back to work); and (3) the desire to liberate men from gender stereo-types. Interestingly, the well-being of children was not among the main reasons for introducing the programme.

What is so special about the parental leave programme as it has developed since 1974? From the parents' point of view it gives unique possibilities for contact with their children, through a series of statutory employment entitlements. It allows *fathers the right to two weeks leave in connection with the birth of their child,* paid at 90 per cent of normal earnings. This 'paternity leave' enables fathers to take care of other children in the family while mothers are in hospital and allows the whole family to spend a week 'adjusting' to the newest member.

The programme also permits parents, fathers as well as mothers, to take *18 months parental leave.* Twelve months leave is compensated at 90 per cent of earnings, a further 3 months is paid at a low, flat-rate level (approximately £6 a day) and the final 3 month period is unpaid. Parental Leave can be taken in one block of time, or several shorter blocks, and at any time until a child is 4. It can also be taken full-time or part-time, and if taken part-time, the length of leave is extended proportionately. Parents can decide between themselves whether one parent will take all of it or whether to divide it and, if so, how. The only constraint is that both parents cannot claim paid leave at the same time; for example, a mother could take 6 months paid leave, followed by the father taking 6 months paid leave – but they could not both take 6 months paid leave at the same time.

A number of other countries in Europe have introduced a system of parental leave. But Sweden is unique in the flexibility of provision and the level of financial compensation made to parents on leave; in most countries, leave is either unpaid or paid at a low level. One consequence of this leave is that practically all Swedish children are at home with one of their parents until they are at least 12 months old.

Finally, the parental leave programme contains two other provisions, the purpose of which are to make it easier for employed parents to combine parenthood and employment. Parents may take up to *90 days leave per year per child until he or she is 12, to provide care if the child is ill,* to take the child for health check-ups or if the person who normally provides for the child is ill or infectious; since 1980, the average period of leave taken per child has been stable at just over six days a year. In addition, parents may take *two 'contact days' per child per year;* this is intended to enable parents to spend a few days with their children in day care facilities or schools, to become acquainted with the activities carried on and to have informal contact with the staff. Both types of leave are paid at 90 per cent of earnings (with benefit payments, as with payments for other types of leave, coming from State-run social insurance funds); and in both cases, both mothers and fathers are eligible to take leave and can decide how to allocate the leave period.

As well as these rights to various types of paid leave, legislation gives parents the right to work reduced hours – 6 hours a day or a 25 per cent reduction in full-time working hours – until the end of the child's first year at school, although without any compensation for lost earnings. Both parents can take advantage of this entitlement if they choose.

In order to promote parental leave, and especially the taking of leave by fathers, nationwide advertising campaigns were launched during the 1970s picturing wrestlers, soccer players and other masculine men holding, feeding and strolling babies. Despite these efforts to promote fathers taking leave, the numbers are still rather low. Ten per cent take advantage of parental leave during the first 6 months after birth; generally, mothers breast-feed babies for the greater part of this period so it is possible that fathers do not wish to compete during this period. During the next 3 month period, around 28 per cent of men take leave for some part of this time.

Take-up by fathers of other types of leave is rather higher. In particular 83 per cent take paternity leave, averaging 9 of the 10 days available. Among parents taking time off to care for sick children, 41 per cent were fathers and they accounted for 35 per cent of all days of leave taken. While 34 per cent of parents taking advantage of 'contact days' were men.

Fathers experience of parental leave

Some of the consequences of fathers taking, or not taking, parental leave have been explored in a number of recent studies undertaken by myself and colleagues. In one study of 50 men who had been on parental leave, the average length of leave was 4.7 months, and about two-thirds were satisfied with the amount of time they had taken. Most of them, however, were surprised that caring for their young child was so time-consuming and such hard work. The problems they mentioned often had to do with adjustments to the child's rhythm and the difficulties of planning the day; as one father commented, 'at work at least I knew when the coffee break was!'. A common complaint was that they felt lonely and isolated; they had no contact with other fathers on leave and it did not seem right to associate with mothers on leave. Many missed their social contacts at work.

BARNLEDIG PAPPA!

Javisst! Man delar ju på föräldraledigheten.

For most of the men, however, the leave of absence was a positive experience. They felt they had a chance to follow their child's development. Several found it valuable at a personal level and that it put their work into perspective. Some felt they had come to a better understanding of the situation of the average mother and housewife.

What did the women think of sharing the leave? Interestingly enough, almost all mothers were satisfied with having the men stay at home. Each felt her husband was able to participate in caring for the child in a different way than he could otherwise. One woman recounted her experience as follows: 'I remember so well when my husband said "of course we'll divide the first

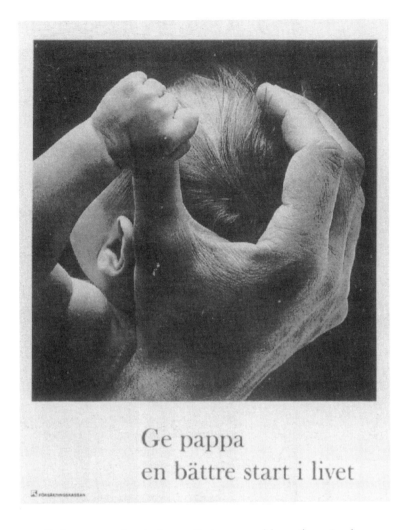

Ge pappa
en bättre start i livet

year". It was so nice to know that we would continue to share the responsibility just as we had done with the housework during the two years we had lived together'.

The effects of parental leave

What are the effects of men staying at home and taking care of their children? One way of answering this question is to compare families where the father goes out to work and the mother is at home taking care of the children, with families where the father is on leave and takes the major responsibility for the child while the mother goes out to work. Some years ago, we completed two studies of this kind.

In the first study, our subjects were 52 middle-class couples, all recruited to the sample while expecting their first child. Half of the fathers initially planned to take at least a month of paid parental leave. Several changed their minds, for various reasons, so that in the end only 17 actually took leave. The average amount of time away from work for these fathers was about 3 months, and leave generally began at the time their child was weaned at about 5 months after the birth.

Although the sample was small and the results must therefore be interpreted cautiously, our findings were surprising. One of our main objectives was to see what effects major responsibility for child care had on parental behaviour towards the child. Observations before, during and after the time when fathers were at home with the child produced very similar results. In general, there were no differences between fathers who stayed at home and fathers who worked; in other words, in relation to the children it did not matter if the father stayed at home or not. On the other hand, we found major differences between the fathers and mothers, regardless of who had been at home and who had been out at work (Hwang 1981, Frodi et al. 1982).

Observations of behaviour when the child was 8 and 16 months produced especially clear differences. Regardless of whether or not the mothers were employed, mothers were consistently more affectionate towards their children than fathers were. They talked to them, smiled and laughed more often; they performed more activities to care for the child; and they held the child more than the fathers did (Hwang 1981, Lamb et al. 1982).

Our second goal was to examine the effects of increased paternal participation on infant preferences for mothers and fathers. As before, the results showed no differences between fathers who stayed at home or remained at work. But the children showed clear-cut preferences for their mothers regardless of the extent to which the fathers had been involved in their care (Lamb et al. 1983). Finally, when the children were one year old, we observed them with their parents in a standardized laboratory procedure designed to assess the quality of infant-parent attachment. We found that the children showed a close and secure attachment to the father as often as to the mother; and that there was no difference between 'home' fathers and employed fathers (Lamb et al. 1982).

We obtained similar results when we studied a new group of fathers on parental leave. We found, once again, that when the mother was present, there were no major differences between what 'home' fathers and employed fathers did with their children. Interestingly, though, the results changed when the fathers were alone with their children. When the mothers were not present, the fathers on parental leave were more anxious than employed fathers to take care of their children (change nappies etc); the employed fathers, on the other hand, spent more time cuddling and playing with the children (Hwang 1985). These results are not amenable to simple explanation. One possibility is that 'home' fathers, like mothers, are used to assuming responsibility for child care even if their partner is not present. In a sense these fathers are more likely to share caregiving responsibilities on an equal basis with the mother. Employed fathers, on the other hand, tend to 'help out', while their partners meet the major proportion of caregiving needs.

Swedish fathers' opportunities to be at home and take care of their children seem to have limited impact on how they act towards their children – at least when the mothers are around. However, results from a recent longitudinal study show that the amount of *early* paternal involvement significantly predicts subsequent paternal involvement. Mothers and fathers of 138 first-born were interviewed when the children averaged 16 months and again 12 months later. The results show that fathers of 28 month olds were more involved: (1) when their partners spent more hours in employment; (2) when both parents agreed that fathers should assume a substantial degree of responsibility for various child care chores; and (3) when the fathers had been more involved in child care 12 months earlier (Hwang et al. in press).

Public day care

The preceding discussion of the parental leave programme may appear unrelated to the issue of day care. In Sweden, however, parents' employment entitlements, with their encouragement to fathers to take more responsibility for children, and public day care services are seen as part of an integrated child care system. One consequence of the parental leave scheme, and its gradual extension, is that the age of admission to day care has fallen; very few Swedish children are now placed in child care outside the home during their first year. A second example concerns the legislation to allow parents to work reduced hours. This was motivated by concern with the length of time many children spent in day care; for example, several studies in the 1970s showed that half of all children under 3 in public day care spent more than 9 hours a day away from home. As a result of the legislation, and parents increasingly organising their working hours to minimise the time their children spend away from home, the average time in day care has dropped sharply, with fewer than 40 per cent of children averaging more than 7 hours a day. 'Contact days' are a third example of the connection between day care provision and the parental leave programme.

Because of parental leave, most women with a child under 1 are at home; between 60–65 per cent of women with a child aged 1–2 and 70–75 per cent with a child aged 2–3 are employed (excluding those on parental leave). Just over half of all children under 3 are cared for only by their parents; 34 per cent receive publicly-funded or 'municipal' day care, leaving 13 per cent cared for by relatives or in paid private day care (Table 1). Sweden is unusual (with the exception of other Scandinavian countries) in having more children under 3 cared for in publicly-funded provision than cared for by relatives or paid private day care.

For children aged 0–6, the proportions are 40 per cent cared for by parents, 47 per cent in municipal day care and 13 per cent with relatives or in paid private day care (Table 1) – though these figures underestimate the number of children receiving some type of publicly-funded pre-school service since they exclude children at kindergarten (discussed below).

Table 1

Different types of day care used by pre-school children: Sweden, 1987

Type of day care	Children under 3 years	Children aged 0–6 years*
No day care (at home with parents)	53%	40%
Relatives	3%	3%
Private day care		
In child's home	3%	3%
Outside home	8%	7%
Municipal day care		
Centre day care	19%	29%
Family day care	15%	18%

*Figures do not include children aged 4–6 attending kindergartens.

The different types of provision

'Pre-school' is the term used for all group care run by the local authorities (or 'municipalities'). This includes day care centres ('daghem'), kindergartens ('deltidsförskola') and mothers' clubs ('öppen förskola'). At day care centres, children usually receive full-time care while their parents are employed. They provide for nearly a fifth of children under 3 and nearly a third of all children under school age (Table 1). In mothers' clubs, the municipality provides premises and a preschool teacher to assist parents who are at home with their children, regardless of age. At kindergartens, children are cared for in groups on a part-time basis, most often for 3 hours a day. Kindergarten is intended to function as a preparation for school, and as a supplementary social training for children at home or in family day care. All Swedish children are entitled to places in kindergartens from their sixth birthday, but many municipalities offer places when children are only 4 or 5 years old (it should be noted that attendance at this form of provision is not included in Table 1).

Most municipalities also support family day care, provided by women who are paid to take care of non-related children in their own homes; this municipal family day care is used by 15 per cent of children under 3 and 18 per cent of all pre-school children (Table 1). Within the municipal system, these 'dagmammas' (childminders) are recruited, paid, supervised and supported by the municipality, which also arranges placements of children.

The most common form of private day care is private 'dagmammas'. They provide the same type of care as municipal family day care homes, except the parents pay the childminder directly (usually without the knowledge of the tax authorities) and the municipality plays no part in regulating the quality of care.

There are also parent cooperatives and day care centres run by various religious or secular associations. In the case of parent co-operatives, a number of parents get together, rent premises and employ one or more pre-school teachers. The relationship between these co-operatives and the municipal day care system varies between municipalities. The co-operatives and other non-profit private centres get municipal grants, but some municipalities give a grant for each place, others give a start-up grant plus a rent allowance and others fund the costs of a certain number of employees. In most cases, the municipality itself is the employer of day care centre staff and operates a 'joint queue' system in which there is. one waiting list and parents are offered places for their children in either municipal or parent co-operative centres, depending on where vacancies first occur. In other cases, the parent co-operative centres are run quite independently.

In Table 1, these types of day care are grouped under the heading of 'private care outside the home'. This also includes a very few day care centres run on a private enterprise basis.

Some children are cared for by nannies in the child's own home (included in the Table under the heading of 'private care in the home'). Some nannies live in, but most only come in during the day. Finally, a relatively small proportion of children (less than 5 per cent) are cared for by relatives, either in the child's home or the relative's home.

The implementation, orientation and quality of Swedish day care

The Pre-school Educational Programme, published in 1987, clearly defines the responsibilities of national and local authorities. The National Board of Health and Welfare has responsibility for all pre-school services and allocates state grants for day care services to the municipalities. The council in each municipality is responsible for the development of public day care in accordance with national guidelines. According to a 1985 law, all municipalities should increase public day care to ensure that by 1991 there is provision for all children over 18 months who need day care. In summer 1990, however, only 67 per cent of municipalities indicated that they would be able to achieve this requirement.

The National Board of Health and Welfare is the central government authority for all social and medical questions and has responsibility nationally for all day care services in the public sector. Because of their reliance on this Board, rather than the Board of Education, day care services have always been more connected with and influenced by ideas and values in the public health sector rather than by goals in the public school sector, and traditionally there has been a reluctance to introduce too much school-like activities into day care centres and kindergartens. While there remains a concern to avoid becoming like schools, the Swedish pre-school services have an explicit educational function; as defined in the National Board's Pre-school Educational Programme, the objective of these services is to 'combine the tasks of providing good educational support for children's development as well as good care and supervision ... Pre-schools should offer goal-oriented and planned educational activities ... (and) good, secure and loving care and companionship'.

The National Board of Health and Welfare has issued central guidelines to guarantee that the expansion of municipal day care centres meets certain quality requirements. The effects of these guidelines have been unmistakable. Swedish day care centres are of high quality with respect to formal or structural aspects of quality.

Design of premises for day care centres

The National Board has defined physical requirements to be met by day care centres. The guidelines were detailed to guarantee that the expansion of day care was not achieved at the expense of quality. As a result, all Swedish centres contain child-sized furniture and fittings, have a room for gross motor activity, a room for more sedentary and fine motor activity, a corner for games involving water and a 'cosy corner' where the children can sit quietly and look at books etc. Most foreign visitors are struck by how well the premises of Swedish day care centres meet their purpose.

Staffing and staff training for day care centres

Staff working with children between the ages of 0 and 6 must, in principle, have completed training either as a children's nurse or a pre-school teacher. To train as a children's nurse, it is necessary to have completed compulsory education (9 years of schooling) and be at least 16 years old. The course lasts two years and provides pupils with basic knowledge of child nursing and development. The pre-school teacher education is a post-secondary course of study that lasts 2½ years. Pupils must be at least 18 years, with 11 years of schooling, and many start the course after successfully completing the children's nurse course.

| Size of groups and adult:child ratios in day care centres | Day care centres vary considerably in size. Typically, they have 3 or 4 groups and around 50–60 children. The availability of places for children under 3 in centres varies between municipalities. Some provide no places for this age group. Most, however, provide for this age group either in 'toddler groups' or 'extended sibling groups'.

In 'toddler groups', all the children are under 3 or 4 years old. Since the youngest child is generally 15–18 months, this means that all children are close to each other in age. The guidelines issued by the National Board of Health and Welfare stipulate that toddler groups should consist of 10–12 children with 4 staff, of which two should be pre-school teachers and two should be children's nurses. Until only a few years ago, this was by far the most common grouping for children under 3.

In 'sibling groups', children are between 3 or 4 and 6 years old. The group contains 15–18 children and 3 staff, 2 teachers and a nurse. 'Extended sibling groups' span the whole pre-school age range; they should contain no more than 15 children, and have at least 3 members of staff. This type of grouping has become more common in recent years. |

| New methods for the regulation of municipal day care | During the 1980s, a rapid process of deregulation of public day care has taken place. State regulation has shifted towards general guidelines governing municipal day care services, combined with support for research and development. In the Pre-school Educational Programme, which is the most recent example of national standards and guidelines regulating the expansion of public day care in Sweden, this shift of focus is clearly expressed, as is the shift in responsibility from the national to the local level (National Board of Health and Welfare 1987). |

| **Municipal family day care** | In 1970, there were 31,000 municipally employed childminders in family day care, caring for 44,000 children. In 1985, approximately the same number of childminders (34,000) looked after 162,000 children. Working as a childminder has developed into a profession – 'dagbarnvrdare' (literally, daychild care provider) – and an increasing number of childminders are working full-time. Previously, childminders were paid according to the number of children they cared for and the number of hours each child was in care; they received no payment if a child was away, for example because of illness. Now they receive a fixed monthly salary.

However, childminders have to look after more children to earn an adequate salary. While a fixed monthly salary may be preferable, it is conditional on the childminder looking after at |

least four unrelated children full-time or providing an equivalent number of hours care for children attending part-time; indeed, many childminders must look after 8–10 part-time children to qualify for their salaries. One of the reasons why childminders enroll so many children on a part-time basis is that many municipalities exclude part-time attendance at day care centres, arguing that places at these centres are too expensive to be filled part-time only.

In a recent survey on family day care homes, childminders averaged 38 years of age and had been employed, on average, for 6.3 years. Most (75 per cent) had their own young children at home, and 60 per cent felt that the great advantage of being a childminder was that they were able to stay at home with their own children. The survey also showed that the childminders looked after an average of 6.4 children, including their own, and that children under three years old spent an average of 30 hours per week in family day care homes (National Board of Health and Welfare 1988).

Municipal family day care homes are part of a municipality's day care provisions and should therefore, in principle, be regulated and controlled in the same way as day care centres, except that a municipally employed family day care home assistant has the responsibility and authority held by the supervisor at a day care centre. The main responsibilities of the family day care home assistant are to investigate, assess and choose childminders, place children, provide childminders with guidance, advice and support, organise and coordinate childminders' activities and develop activities for childminders and children. It is increasingly common for 4 to 6 childminders in the same area to bring their children together regularly in special premises, for example in mothers' clubs or in day care centres. These group activities take place once a week or so, and make it possible to organize games and activities that might be unsuitable in family day care homes. Since the children get to know other childminders and children in these groups, it is easier to substitute if a childminder is ill or otherwise needs to take time off.

Because family day care is usually carried out in the childminder's own home, the quality varies enormously even though municipal day care assistants must approve childminders and ensure that they meet certain minimum requirements. Childminders are also given equipment grants to buy toys etc., and in many municipalities, 50 to 100 hours of introductory training is being introduced. According to the recommendations of the National Board, childminders 'should all, in the long run, have a training equivalent to a children's nurse'.

The detailed regulation of the expansion of day care centres contrasts sharply with the almost total absence of central guidelines governing family day care. Although state grants for municipal family day care were first introduced in 1968, only lately has the central supervisory authority, the National Board of Health and Welfare, involved itself in trying to regulate and develop family day care. Unfortunately, the Board has become involved at a time when the ability to act firmly at national level is very limited; it is no longer possible to issue binding directives and peremptory regulations such as was the case with the expansion of day care centres in the 1970s.

Financing Swedish day care

In the view of the national authorities, day care is a right that, in principle, may be enjoyed by all families with children if they so wish. Consequently, the cost to the individual families of obtaining places in day care services must not be so high as to deter them from exercising this right. This has led to a heavy reliance on public funds to finance day care.

The cost for places in municipal day care centres is divided so that the State and the municipality each contribute just under half, while parents pay an average of 10–15 per cent of the real costs (which in 1987 were 62,400 SEK per place per year or approximately £6,000). The State's contribution to the cost of places in family day care homes is rather less, leaving the municipality to pay just over half the total costs (which in 1987 were 54,100 SEK per place per year) (Swedish Association of Local Authorities 1987). In addition to municipally-run centres and family day care homes, grants are also given to day care centres run by parent co-operatives or non-profit private associations. Other forms of day care that are not supervised by the authorities receive no public funding.

The State's share of day care costs is covered by the so-called 'child care charge' which is part of the social insurance contribution that *all* employers have to pay to the Government (the charge comes to just under 3 per cent of payroll). Municipalities' share of costs comes from municipal taxes levied on companies and individuals.

One effect of the financing system, which has been sharply criticized by the political opposition, is that families using municipal day care are heavily subsidized – whereas families who choose, or are forced, to make their own care arrangements receive no support either from the State or municipalities. This has become a major issue because municipal day care is used more by higher income families and families living in the major cities, and less by families from lower socio-economic backgrounds and families living in rural areas.

Part Two – Research on day care in Sweden

As just described, Sweden has national regulations and norms for staffing levels and training, group size, daily routines and the design of the day care environment. This does not mean, of course, that all day care centres are identical. Indeed, there are large variations in group composition, atmosphere and the staff's experience and working methods; but these variations are within certain specified limits. If we compare day care centres and ordinary homes, it seems probable that variations between different home environments are much larger than between different environments in day care centres (Gunnarson et al. 1987). The homogeneity in day care environments makes Sweden a comparatively easy country in which to undertake day care research. As the number of studies is relatively large, I shall concentrate on describing recent longitudinal research involving comparisons of different types of day care.

One of the most comprehensive longitudinal studies was carried out by Moncrieff Cochran and Lars Gunnarsson (Cochran 1977, Gunnarsson 1978, Larner 1982, Cochran and Gunnarsson 1985). Their research focussed on 60 children who had been in centre day care since they were 12 months old. Their development at five years of age was compared with that of 60 children who had been cared for either at home or in family day care, and another follow-up study was carried out when the children were 9 to 10 years old (Larner 1982). One problem with this study is that no distinction is made between children cared for at home by their parents and cared for by childminders, while children in centre day care were only studied in their centre environments and children cared for at home were only studied in their home environments.

At the age of one, no differences were observed between the children themselves or in the emotional closeness between children and their mothers. The results obtained in the later follow-up studies showed very small differences between the groups. Indeed *between* group differences were much smaller than differences *within* groups. Sex differences were most pronounced. Girls cared for at home were more 'obedient', while girls in day care centres were more likely to manipulate adults in order to get their way. In this respect girls with day care centre experience were similar to boys cared for at home. The boys in centre day care were by far the most peer-oriented group, and they had very little contact with adults.

The 'Gothenburg Child Care Project', undertaken by Michael Lamb and myself together with colleagues at Gothenburg University, was set up to assess the effects of out-of-home care on various aspects of children's social, personality and intellectual development, in the context of other important life events and family circumstances (see, for example, Hwang et al. 1988). Among the potential influences considered were the nature and quality of in-home and out-of-home care, perceived social support, various indices of socio-economic status and reports of the children's temperament. Of the 145 children in the study, none had begun out-of-home care before they were visited by the research team at an average age of 16 months. Children were divided into three groups: those who were to begin in centre-based day care (N=53); those who were offered care in municipal family day care homes or where parents made their own arrangements with private childminders (N=33); and finally a group which did not enter day care (N=59). All children were visited in their homes on six occasions, twice every year when they were, on average, 16, 28 and 40 months old. In addition, children in the different day care groups were visited three times in their out-of-home care settings.

Overall, the results showed no effects of type of care on social, emotional or intellectual development. The most important factors in shaping children's development were the quality of care in their own homes, especially the 'emotional climate' of the family. Rather surprisingly, socio-economic factors were of little importance. Some of the structural measures of the quality of alternative care were also predictive of child outcome. These measures included (1) group size (the fewer the children, the better the outcome); (2) child: staff ratio (the fewer the children per adult, the better the outcome); (3) age mixture and age range (the narrower the age range and the more same aged peers, the better the outcome).

The only longitudinal Swedish study that reports distinctive differences between children with different day care histories is by Bengt-Erik Andersson and his colleagues at Stockholm University (Andersson 1986, 1989). The sample consisted of 128 children, who were 3 years old when the study began. In later contacts, when the children were nearly 8 and 13 years old, their teachers were asked to assess their cognitive and social competence. Children with early experiences of out-of-home care, whether in centres or family day care, had developed more favourably (both socially and cognitively) than children cared for exclusively at home or children who began in out-of-home care after their second birthday. The most pronounced positive effects were shown by children who began out-of-home care prior to their first birthday.

In sum, Swedish longitudinal research studies on the effects of day care on children's development' have, with one exception, not demonstrated any enduring effects of day care per se or type of day care on children's subsequent development – and the one exception found early day care experience associated with positive effects. Quality of care, both at home and in day care settings, seems to be a more important determinant of later development than type of care experienced by children.

Conclusion

So far, I have concentrated mainly on the positive aspects of Swedish day care. Most children above the age of three, and a substantial proportion of children under three, are able to receive public day care. It is generally of very high quality and affordable for parents. Children attending day care develop at least as well as children cared for at home. Day care policy is supported by and integrated with an extensive system of employment entitlements for parents, which increase their opportunities to provide care for their children.

In conclusion however I would like to point to a few shortcomings in Swedish day care:

1. **Limited choice:** One might argue that Swedish parents have a limited choice of out-of-home care. The policy makers in Sweden are strongly in favour of public day care. Other forms of provisions that are not supervised by the authorities do not receive public funding.

2. **Too much homogeneity:** Although Swedish public day care is of high quality, it is also very homogeneous. Most day care centres look alike and the curriculum is very similar. There is little room for ideas that are out of the ordinary. (In neighbouring Denmark, where there is also a very extensive system of publicly funded day care, centres have much greater autonomy and there is consequently more heterogeneity).

3. **Regional and political variation:** There are large variations between different parts of the country, both in the total quantity of public day care and the division between centre and family day care. In large cities, municipal day care is well developed and the emphasis is on centre day care. In these areas, levels of day care are not related to whether municipalities are governed by right or left wing parties. In other parts of the country, high levels of municipal day care are only found in industrial towns with a stable left wing majority.

4. **Use of public day care services:** There are proportionately fewer children of immigrant parents in public day care. There also exists a clear connection between parents' educational level and employment status and use of public day care. Parents with higher education and higher social status place their children earlier in out-of-home care and are more positive about day care, especially centre day care for young children. So, for centre day care there exists a strange paradox in Sweden. On the one hand, the Social Democratic Party argues strongly in favour of centre day care; on the other hand, the backbone of their support, the working class, are substantially under-represented in municipal day care.

The reason for this differential use of day care is subject to much discussion. Some emphasize the non-availability of municipal day care for parents whose jobs do not have regular 9–5 hours. Others emphasize attitudes towards day care among the working class. Data from my own work suggest it is mainly the latter reason. Swedish working class parents are less positive about others taking care of their young children. Instead they emphasize a desire to be close to their children and mould their development, and are doubtful about group care at an early age (Broberg and Hwang 1985).

A concluding remark, returning to the introduction to this paper. Geoffrey Levy may be right about us Swedes. We may be lazy, unable to enjoy the good things in life – and have bad cars. Our family policy programme, however, is among the most extensive in the world, and despite some shortcomings, I believe that it satisfies the needs of most Swedish parents and children.

References

Andersson, B-E. (1986). 'Home care or external care? A study of the effects of public child care on children's development when 8 years old'. *Reports on Education and Psychology, No. 2,* Stockholm University Institute of Education.

Andersson, B-E. (1989). 'Effects of public day care – a longitudinal study'. *Child Development, 60,* 857–867.

Broberg, A. & Hwang, C. P. (1985). 'Vilken barntillsyn har Småbarnsföräldrar och vilken vill de ha?' In L. Gunnarsson (ed.) *Symposiet Vrd Fostranundervisning Del 3, Relationen-Familj institutionen.* Publikationer frn Institutionen fr pedagogik, Gteborgs universitet: 18.

Cochran, M. M. (1977). 'A comparison of group day care and family child-rearing patterns in Sweden'. *Child Development, 48,* 702–707.

Cochran, M. M. & Gunnarsson, L. (1985). 'A follow-up study of group day care and family based childrearing patterns'. *Journal of Marriage and the Family, 47,* 297–309.

Frodi, A. M., Lamb, M. E., Hwang, C. P. and Frodi, M. (1982). 'Father-mother infant interaction in traditional and non-traditional Swedish families: a longitudinal study'. *Alternative Lifestyles, 1,* 3.32.

Gunnarsson, L. O. (1978). 'Children in day care and family care in Sweden: a follow-up'. *Research Bulletin, No. 21,* Department of Education. Göteborg: Göteborg Universitet.

Gunnarsson, L., Andersson B-E. & Cochran, M. (1987). 'Barnomsorg utanför hemmet – forskning kring utvecklingseffekter'. In H. Dahlgren, L. Gunnarsson and G. Kärrby (eds.) *Barnets väg genom förskola, skola och in i vuxenlivet.* Lund: Studentlitteratur.

Hwang, C. P. (1981). *Parent-infant interaction during the first eight months of life.* Doctoral thesis, Gteborg universitet.

Hwang, C. P. (1986). 'The behaviour of Swedish primary and secondary caretaking fathers in relation to mothers' presence'. *Developmental Psychology, 22,* 749–751.

Hwang, C. P., Elden, G. & Fransson, C. (1984). 'Arbetsgivares och arbetskamraters attityder till pappaledighet'. *Rapport frn Psykologiska institutionen, nr. 1.* Göteborg: Göteborg universitet.

Hwang, C. P., Lamb, M. E. & Broberg, A. (1989). 'The development of social and intellectual competence in Swedish pre-schoolers'. In K. Kreppner and R. M. Lerner (eds.) *Family system and lifespan development*. Hillsdale, NJ.: Erlbaum.

Hwang, C. P., Lamb, M. E. & Broberg, A. (in press). 'Associations between parental agreement regarding child-rearing and the characteristics of families in Sweden'. *International Journal of Behavioural Development*.

Lamb, M. E., Hwang, C. P., Frodi, A. M. and Frodi, M. (1982). 'Security of mother- and father-infant attachment and stranger sociability of traditional and non-traditional Swedish families'. *Infant Behaviour and Development, 5,* 355–367.

Lamb, M. E., Frodi, A. M., Hwang, C. P., Frodi, M. & Steinberg, J. (1982). 'Mother- and father-infant interaction involving play and holding in traditional and non-traditional Swedish families'. *Developmental Psychology, 18,* 215–222.

Lamb, M. E., Frodi, M., Hwang, C. P. & Frodi, A. M. (1983). 'Effects of paternal involvement on infant preferences for mothers and fathers'. *Child Development, 54,* 450–459.

Larner, M. (1982). *Effects of day care on social development.* Unpublished paper, Cornell University.

National Board of Health and Welfare (1987). *Pedagogiska program för förskolan. Allmänna råd från Socialstyrelsen 1987:3.* Stockholm: Allmänna förlaget.

National Board of Health and Welfare (1988). *Kommunala familjedaghem. Allmänna råd från Socialstyrelsen 1988:4.* Stockholm: Allmänna förlaget.

Swedish Association of Local Authorities (1987). *Svensk Barnomsorg; en dyrgrip?* Stockholm; Svenska Kommunförbundet.

Day Care Policy and Provision in Britain

Peter Moss

Introduction

Research findings must always be set in context. Without doing that, it is difficult to interpret their meaning and impossible to assess their generalisability and wider significance. Among the most relevant aspects of that context are the policy framework and system of provision within which research occurs. This paper describes that context for under 5s services in Britain and sets the scene for the subsequent chapter by Edward Melhuish on British day care research. It covers all forms of provision for children under 5, including education as well as day care services.

Day care and education policy for children under 5

Perhaps the most striking feature of British policy on day care and education services for under-fives since the War has been its consistency. In nursery education, growth was deliberately constrained for reasons of public expenditure until the 1972 Education White Paper (Department of Education 1972). This policy statement proposed a period of rapid expansion so that 'within the next 10 years nursery education should become available without charge . . . to those children whose parents wish them to benefit from it'; it was estimated that this would involve provision for 50 per cent of 3 year olds and 90 per cent of 4 year olds.

This target has never been met. Public expenditure crises in the 1970s checked growth and during the 1980s the target was abandoned. The 1985 Education White Paper (Department of Education 1985) spelt out a new policy, to maintain the status quo – 'The Government will make it its aim that plans for local authority expenditure should allow provision (for under fives) to continue in broad terms within broadly the same total as today'. Recently, the Government has approved increased expenditure on nursery education, partly in response to the rising numbers of 3 and 4 year olds but also to 'permit a further real increase in participation rate' (House of Commons Committee on Education 1989a). It is not clear what growth this increased expenditure will permit, and there is no suggestion of re-adopting the White Paper objective of nursery education for all 3 and 4 year olds whose parents want it.

The other aspect of education policy for under-fives which must be mentioned is the admission of 4 year olds to primary school. The main growth of this provision occurred in the 1960s, when the number of 4 year olds in primary school doubled. Numbers peaked in 1975, at 266,000, then fell somewhat to 200,000 in 1982, since when they have increased again to over 250,000.

If we turn to services for under-fives outside the education system, post-war policy has been based on two main principles. First, publicly-funded provision of day care has been confined to children deemed to be in need. With the exception of lone parents, parental employment has not been regarded as a priority need for admission to such provision; over the years increasing priority has been given to children from disturbed backgrounds and who are considered by social workers to be 'at risk'. Second, the Government has assumed some responsibility for the regulation of private services, through the agency of local authorities.

Both principles are reaffirmed in the 1989 Children Act. Under the Act, local authority Social Services Departments have a general *duty* to provide day care 'as appropriate for pre-school children in need', and *discretion* to provide such services for other children; given the very tight controls on local authority expenditure, few will be able to exercise this discretion to any significant extent. Regulation of the private sector will be by registration, inspection and a 3 yearly review of all day care provision to be conducted jointly by Social Services and Education Departments.

If day care policy has remained unaltered in essence, the explicit justification for the policy has undergone some change in emphasis. Both the 1945 and 1968 Ministry of Health Circulars (221/45 and 37/68) emphasised that younger pre-school children *should* be at home with their mothers; this was deemed to be in the child's best interest on the basis of unattributed expert opinion. Older pre-school children would be expected, in the normal course of events, to use nursery schooling or similar provision.

These documents, and the policy they informed, assumed that day care was an essentially private matter, except in exceptional circumstance. This view has become more explicit in the 1980s. In its evidence to the House of Commons Education Committee in 1989, the Department of Health asserted that 'in the first instance it is the responsibility of the parents to make arrangements, including financial arrangements, for the day-care of pre-school children' (House of Commons Education Committee 1989b).

This belief in private, parental responsibility for day care has determined the Government's response to the current rapid changes in need and demand as more women enter employment. Parents are expected to make arrangements for day care either through their own social networks or by buying services in the private market. Employers may also assume some responsibility for employees' day care needs, where they consider it necessary for labour force or other economic reasons. The Ministerial Group on Women's Issues has said that 'employers have a significant part to play to provide childcare facilities and attract skilled mothers who have chosen to work in a time of demographic change'. Public involvement, either in funding or providing provision, is firmly ruled out; the Government's role is confined to regulating private provision and to encouraging others (for example employers and school governors) to make provision.

The clear objective of policy therefore is to encourage a private market in under 5s services, paid for by parents (sometimes with the support of employers), and only diluted by a limited amount of State nursery education and very small quantities of public day care for children 'in need'. The Government want to see the market provide diversity, choice and good quality. Issues of access, equality and segregation receive no attention.

Before leaving this review of daycare policy, one other feature should be noted. Despite being unwilling to fund or provide service for employed parents, there has been a consistent interest by successive Governments in the improvement of private childminding. Local authorities have been encouraged to increase levels of support and limited sums of money have been given for innovatory projects. Childminding has received official support for several reasons including its perceived 'low cost' and 'flexibility'. It has also been supported as the type of care considered to be closest to the ideal, that is the child cared for by its mother at home, and because there has been a prevalent view that children under 3 are too young to benefit from group care.

Day care and education provision for children under 5

The present pattern of service provision

This brief policy background helps to explain the present pattern of service provision for children under 5 and recent developments in this provision. **Playgroups** are the most important form of provision, in terms of numbers of places and numbers of children attending; they provide places equivalent to about 13 per cent of the under 5s population or about a third of all 3 and 4 year olds (Table 1). This mainly private service developed initially to fill the gap created by a lack of nursery education: but the playgroup movement now regards playgroups as a permanent feature, with a distinct and valuable identity, and as 'a major provider of pre-school education'.

Next come two forms of educational provision. **Nursery education** provides places for just under 10 per cent of under 5s or roughly a quarter of 3 and 4 year olds, **reception classes** for only slightly fewer children. **Childminders** provide places for 6 per cent of children under 5, while **local authority** and **private nurseries** provide for about 1 per cent each (Table 1).

Table 1

Number of Places in different Under Fives Services: England, 1989

	Number of places (full-time and part-time)(a)	Places per 1,000 children under 5	Number of places (full-time equivalent)	FTE places per 1,000 children under 5
LA nursery education	295,584	95	167,496	54
LA reception class	251,980	81	241,472	78
LA day nurseries/family centres	32,585	11	28,789	9
Private day nurseries	46,589	15	46,589	15
Childminders	186,356	60	186,356	60
Playgroups	406,656	131	162,662(b)	52
Total	1,219,750	393	833,364	269

(a) This column may underestimate the number of places in 'private day nurseries' and 'childminders'; official statistics do not indicate how many registered places in these two types of provision are used on a part-time basis (in which case 1 registered place might be used as 2 part-time places).
(b) Based on playgroups being open on average for 4 half-day sessions per week (PPA 1988), with 10 sessions a week as a full-time equivalent.
Sources: Department of Education, 1990; Department of Health, 1990

These figures need qualification. They count *all places, whether part-time or full-time,* on the same basis. However most provision in playgroups and nursery education is part-time; if we convert these part-time places to full-time equivalents, to give some idea of the *total volume of provision,* then not only does the overall level of provision reduce substantially, but playgroups and nursery education are less prominent, each offering the same volume of provision as childminders. On the same basis, reception class provision becomes the most important under-fives service (Table 1).

On the other hand, figures for places under-estimate the importance of playgroups in terms of *numbers of children using the service.* Most playgroups operate on a part-time basis, with the average playgroup open for four half-day sessions a week; but these places are often shared, so that the average playgroup attendance per child is just two half-day sessions a week. So, although there are places for about 13 per cent of children under 5 in playgroups, in practice about 20 per cent of this age group actually attend (Table 2).

Table 2

Percentage of children attending services by age:
Britain, 1979 and 1986

		Percentage of children attending service, aged (years)					
		0–1	1–2	2–3	3–4	4–5	Total
Maintained school	1979	–	–	*	13	40	11
	1986	–	–	*	12	47	13
Private school	1979	–	–	–	5	5	2
	1986	–	–	2	6	5	3
Day nursery	1979	*	3	5	8	9	5
	1986	1	2	5	12	9	6
Playgroup	1979	*	3	12	39	33	17
	1986	*	2	16	48	32	20
Childminder	1979	3	4	4	3	5	4
	1986	3	5	5	5	2	4
Other	1979						
	1986	1	4	4	3	2	3
Total**	1979	3	6	17	58	78	32
	1986	6	10	26	76	89	42
Number of children	1979	424	363	390	360	393	1,930
	1986	300	320	320	313	340	1,593

– = no children; * = less than 0.5%
** Percentages do not sum to the total as some children may be using more than one type of service.
There is no information for 'other' for 1979.
Source: Moss and Owen, 1990 (based on 1979 and 1986 General Household Survey)

The second qualification is that official statistics do not include some important forms of day care. Nannies and others providing care in children's own homes are a small but growing form of provision. An estimate in 1987 suggested that 30,000 children, or 1 per cent of the under-fives population, were cared for in this way (Cohen 1988), but the number has probably grown substantially since then as more mothers have entered employment. More significant are relatives, in particular grandmothers, who continue to be the main form of non-parental care used by working parents, yet are invariably neglected in policy-making, service provision and official statistics.

Main characteristics of
provision for children
under 5

I want now to consider some of the main characteristics of the
system of under-fives services in Britain. First, there is
undoubtedly diversity, both in the types of provision available –
which include day nurseries, playgroups, childminders, nursery
education and reception class – and in the suppliers of
provision, which include local authorities, various self-help and
voluntary bodies, a few employers and private proprietors. In
having this sort of 'mixed economy' Britain is not particularly
unusual. What marks Britain out from most other countries is
the **low level of public sector involvement** in either providing or
funding services.

Most other countries have, or are actively working towards, 2 or
3 years of publicly-funded nursery education (or kindergarten),
an objective which has been rejected in Britain with the ditching
of the 1972 White Paper targets. Instead, limited nursery
education provision is supplemented by playgroups and early
admission to primary school. These types of provision are found
in substantial numbers in only two other European countries,
Ireland and the Netherlands, both of which have no nursery
education (for a fuller discussion of the role of playgroups in
these three countries, see Lloyd et al. 1989).

While reception class and nursery education provision is publicly
funded, most playgroup provision is not. In 1987, only about a
third of playgroups which were members of PPA reported
receiving any grant, and those that did averaged just £144 or
under 5 per cent of their running costs. For the country as a
whole, PPA has estimated that grants contribute less than 2
per cent of total running costs (Statham et al. 1990). Apart from
nursery education, reception classes and some playgroups,
public funding of under 5s services is confined to a relatively
small number of places in day nurseries (and family centres) and
a smaller number of children whose places in private provision
(at childminders, playgroups or nurseries) are paid for by local
authorities – a total of about 2 per cent of all children under 5.

Overall, and including nursery education and reception classes,
only a fifth of under-fives benefit from any public funding
(Table 3). By contrast, over 40 of under 5s benefit from
publicly-funded services in France, Belgium, Italy, Denmark
and Sweden.

Another way of looking at this issue is to compare the
contribution of services which receive public funds and services
which depend entirely on private funding. Rather less than half
of the children who receive some form of education or day care
provision attend publicly-funded services. Moreover this
proportion is falling (Tables 2 and 4). During the 1980s, the rate
of increase in publicly-funded provision has slowed, while

Table 3

Number of Children provided with Under Fives services by Local Authorities: England. 1989

	Number of children	Number of children per 1,000 children under 5
Day nurseries – la run	32,585	11
privately run	1,823	1
Childminders	5,738	2
Playgroups – local authority run	2,717	1
privately run	11,107	4
School – nursery class or school	295,584	95
reception class	251,980	81
Total	601,534	194

In the case of privately run services, children are placed and paid for by local authorities.

Sources: Department of Education, 1990; Department of Health, 1990

provision in private provision, mainly childminders and private nurseries, has grown very rapidly especially since 1984.

In the five years from 1984–89, places in private nurseries doubled and increased by two-thirds at childminders. By contrast places in nursery education increased by only just over 10 per cent and actually decreased in local authority day nurseries. The exception to this general picture is playgroups, where places hardly increased between 1984 and 1989, and have actually decreased since 1987 (Table 4).

Table 4

Change in Number of Places in different Under Fives Services: England, 1979–89

	1979–1984	1984–1989
LA nursery education		
–children attending	+23%	+14%
–full-time equivalent places	+18%	+11%
LA reception class		
–children attending	+8%	+7%
–full-time equivalent places	+9%	+6%
LA day nurseries		
–children attending	+17%	−4%
–places	+2%	−*
Private nurseries		
–places	+3%	+95%
Childminders		
–places	No information	+60%
Registered playgroups		
–places	+6%	+4%

* = less than 0.5%

Sources: Department of Education, 1990; Department of Health, 1990

A second feature of the system of provision is **its concentration on part-time places.** Three-quarters of children attending some form of under-fives service in 1986 went for five half day sessions or less per week; indeed nearly half went only three half day sessions or less (Table 5). The British system therefore spreads a relatively small volume of service thinly to produce relatively high attendance rates, at least for children aged 3 and 4 over 80 per cent of whom attend some type of service.

Table 5

Frequency of attendance per week for children using services; Britain, 1986

Frequency of attendance	Type of service							
Nursery	Main-tained School	Private School	Day School	Play-group	Child-minder	Other	Total	Mother & Todd-ler
	%	%	%	%	%	%	%	%
1 half day	2	7	13	11	12	46	11	82
2 half days	3	21	14	45	10	2	23	12
3 half days	3	9	9	26	3	–	13	2
4 half days	2	7	2	8	2	5	5	*
5 half days	48	26	38	9	15	–	24	1
1–4 full days	*	2	9	*	28	5	4	1
5 full days	42	21	14	*	25	18	17	–
Other	–	7	2	–	7	25	3	1
Number of children	200	43	95	320	64	46	672	246

– = No children
* = Less than 0.5%
Source: OPCS, 1989

A third feature of the system is **the poor pay and conditions of most of the workers,** in particular childminders and playgroup workers but also many day nursery workers and nannies (Cohen 1988). This contributes to instability in the workforce. There is evidence of high turnover among childminders, with women moving out of the work when their children get older or as better jobs become available (Moss 1987). Turnover is also thought to be high amongst other care workers, including nursery staff and nannies (Cohen 1988). If American experience is a good guide, then this will be an increasing problem.

A fourth feature of the system is **large variations between local authorities.** These variations apply to levels of public and private provision of all types of service (Tables 6–10); the degree of financial support given by local authorities to playgroups; and the resources allocated to the registration, supervision and support of private services (Statham et al. 1990). These large local differences reflect a reluctance of successive Governments to set and enforce either national targets for levels of provision or, in the case of day care, national standards for supervision or support. In the words of John Patten in 1983, when he was a Minister at the Department of Health, 'the level of childcare provision is a matter for local authorities to consider in the light of circumstances prevailing within their area'.

Table 6

Provision of Nursery Education (Full-Time Equivalent Places) per Thousand Children Under 5, by Local Authority:
England, 1989

Local Authority	Rate	Type of Authority	Local Authority	Rate	Type of Authority
Gloucestershire	0	County	Rochdale	68	Metropolitan
Somerset	3	County	Calderdale	69	Metropolitan
Bromley	4	Outer London	Gateshead	69	Metropolitan
Wiltshire	4	Metropolitan	Bedfordshire	71	County
West Sussex	7	County	Dudley	72	Metropolitan
Havering	8	Outer London	Humberside	73	County
Norfolk	9	County	Camden	73	Inner London
Hampshire	10	County	Derbyshire	73	County
Kent	10	County	Leeds	74	Metropolitan
Dorset	11	County	Baling	74	Outer London
Isle of Wight	12	County	Westminster	75	Inner London
Essex	12	County	Brent	75	Outer London
Hereford & Worcester	13	County	Sunderland	76	Metropolitan
East Sussex	14	County	Waltham Forest	78	Outer London
Croydon	15	Outer London	Kirklees	79	Metropolitan
Lincolnshire	17	County	Doncaster	80	Metropolitan
Buckinghamshire	20	County	Merton	80	Outer London
Devon	22	County	Bradford	81	Metropolitan
Surrey	23	County	Durlam	82	County
Redbridge	24	Outer London	Birmingham	84	Metropolitan
Shropshire	24	County	Knowsley	84	Metropolitan
Cambridgeshire	25	County	Tameside	84	Metropolitan
Suffolk	28	County	Lewisham	84	Inner London
Cornwall	29	County	Wandsworth	84	Inner London
Bexley	29	Outer London	Bolton	85	Metropolitan
Oxfordshire	30	County	Lambeth	88	Inner London
Harrow	31	Outer London	Haringey	88	Outer London
Warwickshire	35	County	Hackney	89	Inner London
Lancashire	36	County	Sheffield	89	Metropolitan
Northamptonshire	38	County	Rotherham	91	Metropolitan
Stockport	39	Metropolitan	Hillingdon	92	Outer London
North Yorkshire	39	County	Oldham	93	Metropolitan
Trafford	39	Metropolitan	Kensington	96	Inner London
Enfield	40	Outer London	Wakefield	97	Metropolitan
Richmond-Upon-Thames	41	Outer London	South Tyneside	98	Metropolitan
Cheshire	43	County	Sandwell	98	Metropolitan
Wirral	43	Metropolitan	Nottinghamshire	98	County
Avon	43	County	Barnsley	101	Metropolitan
Cumbria	45	County	Liverpool	104	Metropolitan
Sutton	46	Outer London	Southwark	106	Inner London
Coventry	48	Metropolitan	Greenwich	107	Inner London
Berkshire	50	County	North Tyneside	109	Metropolitan
Wigan	53	Metropolitan	Hammersmith	109	Inner London
Leicestershire	56	County	Cleveland	110	County
Solihull	60	Metropolitan	Newcastle-Upon-Tyne	114	Metropolitan
Kingston-Upon-Thames	60	Outer London	Wolverhampton	114	Metropolitan
Sefton	60	Metropolitan	Newham	115	Outer London
Northumberland	61	County	Islington	115	Inner London
Hertfordshire	61	County	Walsall	121	Metropolitan
Barnet	61	Outer London	Tower Hamlets	145	Inner London
Staffordshire	63	County	Salford	163	Metropolitan
Bury	64	Metropolitan	Manchester	173	Metropolitan
Barking	66	Outer London	Hounslow	194	Outer London
St Helens	66	Metropolitan			

Source: Department of Education and Science, 1990.

Table 7

Places in Local Authority Day Nurseries, per Thousand Children Under 5, by Local Authority:
England, 1989

Local Authority	Rate	Type of Authority	Local Authority	Rate	Type of Authority
Rotherham	0	Metropolitan	Wirral	9	Metropolitan
Isle of Wight	0	County	Avon	10	County
Barnsley	0	Metropolitan	Newcastle-Upon-Tyne	10	Metropolitan
Cornwall	0	County	South Tyneside	10	Metropolitan
Wiltshire	0	Metropolitan	Bolton	10	Metropolitan
Warwickshire	0	County	Sandwell	10	Metropolitan
Norfolk	0	County	Sheffield	10	Metropolitan
West Sussex	0	County	Gateshead	10	Metropolitan
Shropshire	0	County	Kingston-Upon-Thames	10	Outer London
Berkshire	0	County	Havering	11	Outer London
Bromley	0	Outer London	Merton	11	Outer London
North Yorkshire	0	County	Nottinghamshire	11	County
East Sussex	0	County	Leicestershire	12	County
Kent	0	County	Wigan	12	Metropolitan
Suffolk	0	County	Barking	12	Outer London
Dudley	0	Metropolitan	Barnet	13	Outer London
Buckinghamshire	0	County	Hillingdon	13	Outer London
Hertfordshire	1	County	Richmond-Upon-Thames	13	Outer London
Surrey	1	County	Oldham	13	Metropolitan
Humberside	1	County	Newham	14	Outer London
Wakefield	1	Metropolitan	Wolverhampton	14	Metropolitan
Gloucestershire	2	County	Hounslow	15	Outer London
Solihull	2	Metropolitan	Sunderland	15	Metropolitan
Northumlerland	2	County	Bradford	15	Metropolitan
Lincolnshire	2	County	Sefton	16	Metropolitan
Doncaster	2	Metropolitan	Lancashire	16	County
Somerset	3	County	Baling	17	Outer London
Oxfordshire	3	County	Lewisham	17	Inner London
Essex	3	County	Haringey	17	Outer London
Northamptonshire	3	County	Coventry	18	Metropolitan
Hereford & Worcester	3	County	Waltham Forest	18	Outer London
Bexley	3	Outer London	Trafford	18	Metropolitan
Hampshire	3	County	Knowsley	20	Metropolitan
Devon	3	County	Rochdale	20	Metropolitan
Dorset	4	County	North Tyneside	20	Metropolitan
Durham	4	County	Birmingham	20	Metropolitan
Cambridgeshire	4	County	Leeds	24	Metropolitan
Cumbria	5	County	Greenwich	27	Inner London
Redbridge	5	Outer London	Liverpool	27	Metropolitan
St Helens	6	Metropolitan	Salford	29	Metropolitan
Sutton	6	Outer London	Tameside	30	Metropolitan
Staffordshire	6	County	Tower Hamlets	31	Inner London
Calderdale	6	Metropolitan	Camden	37	Inner London
Walsall	7	Metropolitan	Hackney	39	Inner London
Stockport	7	Metropolitan	Manchester	39	Metropolitan
Kirklees	7	Metropolitan	Wandsworth	40	Inner London
Bedfordshire	7	County	Lambeth	41	Inner London
Cleveland	8	County	Southwark	41	Inner London
Harrow	8	Outer London	Brent	47	Outer London
Cheshire	8	County	Hammersmith	48	Inner London
Derbyshire	8	County	Westminster	49	Inner London
Croydon	8	Outer London	Kensington	51	Inner London
Enfield	9	Outer London	Islington	58	Inner London
Bury	9	Metropolitan			

Source: Department of Health, 1990.

Table 8

Places in Registered Childminders per Thousand Children Under 5, by Local Authority: England, 1989

Local Authority	Rate	Type of Authority	Local Authority	Rate	Type of Authority
Knowsley	13	Metropolitan	Wigan	60	Metropolitan
Wolverhampton	13	Metropolitan	Bolton	60	Metropolitan
Sunderland	19	Metropolitan	North Yorkshire	60	County
Cleveland	24	County	Hertfordshire	61	County
Doncaster	26	Metropolitan	Calderdale	61	Metropolitan
Walsall	27	Metropolitan	Staffordshire	62	County
Humberside	31	County	Lancashire	64	County
Tower Hamlets	32	Inner London	Durham	64	County
Liverpool	33	Metropolitan	Hackney	65	Inner London
South Tyneside	33	Metropolitan	West Sussex	65	County
Newcastle-Upon-Tyne	34	Metropolitan	Ealing	65	Outer London
Cornwall	35	County	Avon	65	County
Salford	35	Metropolitan	Rochdale	66	Metropolitan
Sefton	36	Metropolitan	Oxfordshire	66	County
Cumbria	36	County	Hampshire	67	County
St Helens	36	Metropolitan	Islington	67	Inner London
Rotherham	37	Metropolitan	Waltham Forest	67	Outer London
Barking	37	Outer London	Cambridgeshire	67	County
Barnsley	38	Metropolitan	Essex	67	County
Birmingham	39	Metropolitan	Redbridge	68	Outer London
Leeds	39	Metropolitan	Bury	68	Metropolitan
Gateshead	40	Metropolitan	Berkshire	69	County
Newham	40	Outer London	Enfield	70	Outer London
East Sussex	41	County	Sutton	70	Outer London
Bradford	41	Metropolitan	Kent	73	County
Manchester	44	Metropolitan	Leicestershire	74	County
Westminster	44	Inner London	Lewisham	74	Inner London
Southwark	45	Inner London	Somerset	75	County
Havering	45	Outer London	Warwickshire	75	County
Dudley	45	Metropolitan	Wiltshire	75	Metropolitan
Coventry	45	Metropolitan	Buckinghamshire	76	County
Isle of Wight	47	County	Barnet	76	Outer London
Sandwell	47	Metropolitan	Stockport	76	Metropolitan
Devon	47	County	Bromley	77	Outer London
Lincolnshire	49	County	Dorset	78	County
Kensington	49	Inner London	Haringey	78	Outer London
Nottinghamshire	49	County	Cheshire	78	County
Wirral	49	Metropolitan	Sheffield	79	Metropolitan
Kingston-Upon-Thames	51	Outer London	Shropshire	81	County
Camden	51	Inner London	Hillingdon	85	Outer London
Derbyshire	52	County	Norfolk	86	County
Wakefield	52	Metropolitan	Hammersmith	86	Inner London
Suffolk	53	County	Gloucestershire	89	County
Bedfordshire	53	County	Surrey	89	County
Northamptonshire	55	County	Tameside	91	Metropolitan
Greenwich	55	Inner London	Oldham	93	Metropolitan
Lambeth	55	Inner London	Northumberland	94	County
Hounslow	56	Outer London	Harrow	94	Outer London
Hereford & Worcester	56	County	Richmond-Upon-Thames	98	Outer London
Bexley	56	Outer London	Trafford	101	Metropolitan
Merton	57	Outer London	Wandsworth	103	Inner London
North Tyneside	58	Metropolitan	Croydon	107	Outer London
Solihull	58	Metropolitan	Brent	126	Outer London
Kirklees	58	Metropolitan			

Source: Department of Health, 1990.

Table 9

Places in Registered Day Nuseries per Thousand Children Under 5, by Local Authority: England, 1989

Local Authority	Rate	Type of Authority	Local Authority	Rate	Type of Authority
Sunderland	0	Metropolitan	Manchester	12	Metropolitan
North Tyneside	0	Metropolitan	Waltham Forest	12	Outer London
Southwark	0	Inner London	Bexley	12	Outer London
Barking	0	Outer London	leeds	12	Metropolitan
Rotherham	0	Metropolitan	Solihull	13	Metropolitan
Hampshire	0	County	Lewisham	13	Inner London
Isle of Wight	0	County	Norfolk	13	County
Wolverhampton	1	Metropolitan	Leicestershire	13	County
Durham	1	County	Oldham	13	Metropolitan
Barnet	2	Outer London	West Sussex	13	County
Walsall	2	Metropolitan	Humberside	14	County
Northumberland	2	County	Oxfordshire	14	County
Hertfordshire	2	County	Hereford & Worcester	14	County
Knowsley	2	Metropolitan	Newcastle-Upon-Tyne	14	Metropolitan
Barnsley	2	Metropolitan	Ealing	15	Outer London
Sheffield	3	Metropolitan	Cheshire	15	County
Kirklees	3	Metropolitan	Shropshire	15	County
Croydon	4	Outer London	Avon	16	County
Newham	4	Outer London	Kingston-Upon-Thames	16	Outer London
Cornwall	4	County	Berkshire	16	County
Derbyshire	4	County	Bedfordshire	16	County
Enfield	4	Outer London	Sefton	17	Metropolitan
Havering	4	Outer London	Richmond-Upon-Thames	18	Outer London
Wiltshire	5	Metropolitan	Lancashire	18	County
South Tyneside	5	Metropolitan	Cleveland	18	County
St Helens	6	Metropolitan	Birmingham	19	Metropolitan
Dudley	6	Metropolitan	Cambridgeshire	19	County
Wakefield	6	Metropolitan	Bolton	19	Metropolitan
Doncaster	6	Metropolitan	Somerset	19	County
Salford	7	Metropolitan	Bromley	19	Outer London
Harrow	7	Outer London	Trafford	21	Metropolitan
Surrey	7	County	Hillingdon	22	Outer London
Wigan	7	Metropolitan	Gloucestershire	22	County
Lincolnshire	8	County	Redbridge	23	Outer London
Merton	8	Outer London	Hounslow	23	Outer London
Gateshead	8	Metropolitan	Staffordshire	24	County
Essex	8	County	North Yorkshire	24	County
Tower Hamlets	9	Inner London	East Sussex	25	County
Devon	10	County	Liverpool	25	Metropolitan
Dorset	10	County	Lambeth	25	Inner London
Warwickshire	10	County	Haringey	27	Outer London
Rochdale	10	Metropolitan	Bury	27	Metropolitan
Greenwich	10	Inner London	Hackney	27	Inner London
Cumbria	10	County	Northamptonshire	30	County
Bradford	11	Metropolitan	Sutton	36	Outer London
Suffolk	11	County	Calderdale	37	Metropolitan
Stockport	11	Metropolitan	Kent	40	County
Buckinghamshire	11	County	Islington	42	Inner London
Coventry	11	Metropolitan	Brent	49	Outer London
Nottinghamshire	11	County	Camden	75	Inner London
Hammersmith	11	Inner London	Wandsworth	90	Inner London
Sandwell	11	Metropolitan	Westminster	107	Inner London
Wirral	11	Metropolitan	Kensington	145	Inner London
Tameside	12	Metropolitan			

Source: Department of Health, 1990.

Table 10

Places in Registered Playgroups per Thousand Children Under 5, by Local Authority: England, 1989

Local Authority	Rate	Type of Authority	Local Authority	Rate	Type of Authority
Walsall	24	Metropolitan	Durham	113	County
Newham	27	Outer London	Derbyshire	113	County
South Tyneside	35	Metropolitan	Dudley	113	Metropolitan
Tower Hamlets	35	Inner London	Berkshire	113	County
Doncaster	48	Metropolitan	Wigan	115	Metropolitan
Kensington	48	Inner London	Enfield	116	Outer London
Westminster	49	Inner London	Lancashire	116	County
Sunderland	53	Metropolitan	Coventry	117	Metropolitan
Manchester	54	Metropolitan	Stockport	119	Metropolitan
Salford	54	Metropolitan	Avon	122	County
Haringey	56	Outer London	Cheshire	122	County
Sandwell	56	Metropolitan	Hertfordshire	123	County
North Tyneside	58	Metropolitan	Sutton	124	Outer London
Hackney	59	Inner London	Barnet	129	Outer London
Birmingham	59	Metropolitan	Staffordshire	133	County
Lambeth	61	Inner London	Oxfordshire	134	County
Waltham Forest	61	Outer London	Bury	135	Metropolitan
Hammersmith	66	Inner London	Calderdale	136	Metropolitan
Brent	66	Outer London	Bedfordshire	138	County
Bradford	66	Metropolitan	Croydon	140	Outer London
Camden	68	Inner London	Wirral	140	Metropolitan
Lewisham	70	Inner London	Warwickshire	143	County
Wakefield	72	Metropolitan	Harrow	143	Outer London
Islington	72	Inner London	Leicestershire	144	County
Ealing	72	Outer London	Trafford	150	Metropolitan
Bolton	74	Metropolitan	Northamptonshire	153	County
Greenwich	74	Inner London	Havering	154	Outer London
Wolverhampton	76	Metropolitan	Devon	155	County
Kingston-Upon-Thames	77	Outer London	Bexley	157	Outer London
Southwark	78	Inner London	Cambridgeshire	158	County
Knowsley	78	Metropolitan	Suffolk	160	County
Solihull	80	Metropolitan	Cumbria	161	County
Gateshead	81	Metropolitan	East Sussex	166	County
Cleveland	82	County	Shropshire	170	County
Tameside	83	Metropolitan	North Yorkshire	171	County
Barking	83	Outer London	Redbridge	171	Outer London
Wandsworth	84	Inner London	Hampshire	172	County
Liverpool	86	Metropolitan	Essex	175	County
Rotherham	87	Metropolitan	Lincolnshire	183	County
St Helens	87	Metropolitan	Wiltshire	184	Metropolitan
Kirklees	90	Metropolitan	Kent	187	County
Nottinghamshire	90	County	Norfolk	187	County
Hounslow	90	Outer London	Gloucestershire	187	County
Newcastle-Upon-Tyne	93	Metropolitan	Surrey	194	County
Oldham	94	Metropolitan	Dorset	199	County
Rochdale	94	Metropolitan	Cornwall	203	County
Hillingdon	96	Outer London	Hereford & Worcester	205	County
Merton	99	Outer London	West Sussex	211	County
Humberside	99	County	Richmond-Upon-Thames	211	Outer London
Northumberland	103	County	Isle of Wight	212	County
Barnsley	105	Metropolitan	Somerset	218	County
Leeds	107	Metropolitan	Bromley	225	Outer London
Sheffield	111	Metropolitan	Buckinghamshire	256	County
Sefton	112	Metropolitan			

Source: Department of Health, 1990.

A final feature of the system is the **overlap of services for children over 3.** In most countries this age group moves into nursery education or its equivalent. In Britain, they are found, in substantial numbers, in childminders, day nurseries, playgroups, nursery classes and reception classes.

This has a number of consequences. It creates an unstable situation for many 3 and 4 year olds, who often move into playgroup then reception class within a few terms or, in some cases, move through playgroup, nursery class and reception class in the same short period. It produces a segregated set of services. There is a small public day care sector, with a heavy concentration of disadvantaged, disturbed and handicapped children. Children whose parents work longer hours are at childminders, (though some are taken by their childminders to playgroup), and increasingly in private day nurseries; many high income dual earner families use nannies and private nurseries at the top end of the price range. Playgroups provide disproportionately for middle-class children, while nursery education is more often used by working-class children (Moss and Owen 1990).

Finally, there are inconsistencies between services for this age group. Children receiving public day care or nursery education have their costs paid; parents with children in other forms of provision generally pay the full cost. Some services are the responsibility of social welfare agencies, while others come under education and have an explicitly educational orientation. The pay and conditions of workers in different services varies considerably.

This overlapping of services is a consequence of the diversity of services referred to at the beginning of this section. Diversity of provision, it is argued, contributes to a greater freedom of choice for parents in Britain. Diversity clearly is an important condition for choice, but it is not sufficient. Other factors in the British situation constrain choice. Let me mention two. The first constraint is availability. Some types of service, for example publicly-funded childminding schemes (such as are found in substantial numbers in Scandinavia, France, Belgium and Portugal) and group care are simply not available to the general run of working parents.

As mentioned, those services that are available are not evenly distributed, which affects the options available to parents. There is a strong negative correlation between the distribution of playgroup and nursery education; in other words, local authorities with fewest nursery education places have most playgroup places and vice versa (Owen and Moss 1989). Most parents therefore have no real choice between these two types of provision and even fewer have the option of a two year period of nursery education for their child. A recent survey of workplace nurseries found that they were heavily concentrated in the South and in smaller urban areas; cities were losing out (Working for Childcare 1989). Similarly, the distribution of all other types of provision is uneven, with highest levels generally found in London and lowest levels in counties. While these geographical variations partly reflect differences in need and demand, they also reflect economic forces, which concentrate private services in the most prosperous areas with greatest labour shortages, and different levels of political commitment in local authorities to the development of services for under fives.

The other constraining factor on choice is cost. There is no reliable information on the current structure of costs throughout the private sector; the figures presented below therefore are indicative rather than precise. For **playgroups,** P P A estimates that in 1987 parents were charged £1.01 a session, though this sum varied between regions. P P A argues that even such a relatively low sum contributes to some parents moving their children to a free nursery or reception class if and when a place becomes available. The N C M A in 1989 recommended a minimum charge for **childminding** of £40 per week per child, but the actual amount charged varies considerably reflecting factors such as local supply and demand. Pay and conditions for **nannies** also seem to vary considerably for similar reasons, with conditions in local labour markets having a major influence on the going rate. A recent study found that within the North-East 'pay differentials seem to exist: in Newcastle £100 per week is the going rate for an experienced live-out nanny (while) in Durham there seems to be a ceiling of £85–90 per week. In Reading the going rate seems to be £100–120 per week' (Gregson and Lowe 1990).

Private nursery costs are also variable. They depend on such factors as the age group provided for, since under 2s cost more, and location, since accommodation, labour and other costs are higher in some areas than others. Other factors which can vary, depending on the proprietor, include staff pay, conditions and training opportunities, adult:child ratios and standards of accommodation and equipment.

Costs in London are particularly high. Two non-profit nurseries in Central London, recently contracted by T C R O, which take children from a few months old, both charge over £100 a week. A newspaper article about a newly opened nursery in West London reported that 'it will cost over £100 per week for a place ... although the cost of half a dozen highly-qualified staff is high – around £75,000 a year – it is the property costs that are the most significant element in the financial equation'

(Drummond 1989). A 1989 report on providing day care in Docklands, concludedthat the cost per child per week in a 24 place nursery on the Isle of Dogs would be £214; 47 per cent of this was accounted for by accommodation costs (mostly rent and rates), while staff costs contributed 41 per cent, equivalent to nearly £90 a week (Peat Marwick McLintock 1989).

At the other extreme, two nurseries in a shire county, recently contacted by TCRU, both of which only take children from 2 upwards, were charging around £50 a week. Further insight into the cost issue was provided by a mother in the TCRU Day Care Study, who has recently established a private nursery. Her nursery, in one of the Home Counties, takes the full age range of under fives and had been charging £62 a week for all children. At this rate the nursery had been losing money and from March 1990 a new scale of charges has been introduced – £92 a week for under 2s and £80 for over 2s.

This suggests that the cost of private nursery care meeting reasonable standards of staffing, accommodation and equipment is £5,000 a year upwards for a child under 2 in the London area. To put this in context, this compares with school fees of £4,500 a year for a day pupil at a leading public school in North London and with *gross* average earnings for women aged 25–29 in full-time non-manual work of around £10,700 a year.

Three final points should be made on this subject of cost. First, except for nannies, these cost figures are for one child; the cost of services for families with two or more children will be proportionately higher. Similarly, day care costs will take a much higher proportion of household income in a one parent household than in a two parent household. We also do not know the relationship between cost and quality; research evidence, however, suggests that quality is influenced by conditions that involve higher costs, for example staff ratios and training, so that some association between quality and cost might be expected.

Second, most of the costs quoted above are based on poor pay and conditions. Paid playgroup workers and childminders have very low earnings, well below average for women workers, and few have access to the sort of employment benefits taken for granted by many workers, such as paid holidays and sick leave and superannuation (Moss 1987, Cohen 1988, Statham et al. 1990). The research on nannies referred to above concludes that this group of workers generally earn well under the £150 per week low pay threshold. Nursery workers may expect paid holidays and sick leave, but their pay is still below average earnings for women; the estimated cost for the Docklands nursery, quoted above, is based on the annual cost of a nursery worker (including employers' national insurance and superannuation contributions) being £9,600.

The costs quoted also include little or no element for support, career development and other measures likely to improve performance – regular in-service training, time to prepare work and meet with parents, visits from advisers and so on. In other words, the costs quoted at present are for a basic service with minimal working conditions. Even so, the costs to a parent are substantial and clearly put many options beyond the reach of many families.

Finally, and following on from the last point, it seems probable that the costs of day care and other human services will increase substantially in real terms because of the need to improve on current poor pay and conditions if sufficient workers are to be recruited and retained and if quality of service is to be improved.

Conclusion

British provision for under fives undoubtedly has many strengths. British nursery education has a high reputation; playgroups have shown the possibilities for parental involvement; important work has been done in bringing childminders within a legal framework and developing support services for them; there have been imaginative innovations, both by local authorities and private organisations; and the Children Act provides considerable potential for improved supervision of private services. Yet if these strengths are to be built on and further progress is to be made, there must be recognition of the weaknesses in the system. Without this recognition, we face the prospect of increasingly incoherent, fragmented, inequitable and under-resourced provision, marked by diversity but little choice in practice. If these weaknesses are recognised and tackled, we face an altogether brighter prospect, which combines diversity and genuine choice with coherence and equality.

References

Cohen, B: (1988). *Caring for Children: UK National Report to the European Childcare Network.* London: Family Policy Studies Centre.

Department of Education (1972). *Education: A Framework for Expansion (Cmnd. 5174).* London: HMSO.

Department of Education (1985) *Better Schools (Cmnd.9469).* London: HMSO.

Department of Education (1990) *Pupils under five years in each Local Authority in England – January 1989 (Statistical Bulletin 7/90),* London: Department of Education.

Department of Health (1990) *Children's Day Care Facilities at 31 March 1989, England.* London: Department of Health.

Drummond, M. (1989) 'Child care; just whose baby is it?'. *The Guardian, May 1989.*

Gregson, N. & Lowe, M. (1990). *The New Servant Class: The Upstairs-Downstairs of the 1990s.* Paper presented to the Conference of the Institute of British Geographers, Glasgow, January 4 1990.

House of Commons Committee on Education (1989a). *Educational Provision for Under Fives. Observations by the Government and Local Authority Associations.* London: HMSO.

House of Commons Committee on Education (1989b). *Educational Provision for Under Fives, Vol. II.* London: HMSO.

Lloyd, E., Statham, J. & Moss, P. (1989). *Playgroups in Three Countries: TCRU Occasional Paper No. 8.* London: TCRU.

Moss, P. (1987). *A Review of Childminding Research: TCRU Occasional Paper No. 6.* London: TCRU.

Moss, P. and Owen, C. (1990). 'Use of pre-school day care and education 1979–86'. *Children and Society, 3,* 259–273.

OPCS (1989). *General Household Survey, 1986.* London: HMSO.

Owen, C. and Moss, P. (1989). 'Patterns of pre-school provision in English local authorities'. *Journal of Education Policy, 4,* 309–328.

Peat Marwick McLintock (1989). *Childcare in Docklands: making it happen.* Report to the London Docklands Corporation.

Statham, J., Lloyd, E., Moss, P., Melhuish, E. & Owen, C. (1990). *Playgroups in a Changing World.* London: HMSO.

Working for Childcare (1990). *Meeting the childcare challenge: can the market provide?* London: Working for Childcare.

Research on Day Care in Britain
Edward Melhuish

Introduction

The previous chapter described the policy and provision context within which British day care research takes place. This chapter presents the main conclusions from that research. Particular attention is given to the largest and most recent project, the Day Care Project undertaken during the 1980s at the Thomas Coram Research Unit. It begins however with a brief review of other day care work, most of which dates from the 1970s.

Review of research on day care in Britain

Most research on day care has concentrated on childminders and nurseries. Only one project – the TCRU Day Care Project described in the next section – has considered day care provided by relatives, even though this is the type of care used most frequently for children with employed parents. There has been no study of nannies or other caregivers providing care in children's own homes.

An early study by Moore (1975) considered children who had been in day care in the 1950's and focused on homecare versus day care comparisons. Children who had not had day care in their first 5 years were compared with children who had experienced at least one year of day care (for more than 25 hours a week) in this period. Some differences were found between these groups at 6 to 7 years of age and in adolescence. At age 7, boys in the day care group did worse at reading. There were also some apparent personality differences; mothers reported greater fastidiousness and less non-conformity in the group which had had no day care, and they were also rated by a psychologist as less excitable and aggressive and more timid. Similar differences were present in adolescence, when they were also some differences in interests. Moore reported more insecurity and fear at age 6 for children who had had less stable day care.

There are several aspects of this study which make interpretation of results difficult. First, the groups were selected post hoc from a broad community sample and may well have differed systematically on a number of other variables as well as day care; confounding variables may well have affected the results, with an apparent 'day care effect' due to some other factors more common among the day care group of children. Second, the day care group includes children with a great diversity of type and timing of day care experience and, therefore, very different patterns of experience. The reported differences therefore may reflect the effects of a particular pattern of day care experienced by a sub-set of children, rather than some general day care effect.

Other British research on day care has concentrated on children in one type of day care, with most attention given to childminders. Mayall and Petrie (1977) found some evidence that childminders were less responsive than mothers to children. They also found that children cared for by the childminders in their sample did not score very well on assessment of language development. However, subsequent work by Raven (1981) showed that this reflected socio-demographic differences in children who use childminders rather than the effects of childminding itself. Other studies of childminders by Bryant et al. (1980) and Davie (1986) lead to the conclusion that the care provided by childminders varies enormously, and that children will behave differently with the childminder than at home. This does not mean that the children are adversely affected by being with the childminder; rather they behave differently in different surroundings. The diversity amongst childminders has also been illustrated by an interview study by Shinman (1981) who investigated the range of childminding provided in an inner London borough (for a fuller account of research on childminding, see Moss 1987).

Studies of nurseries in Britain are few, small-scale and limited in scope. Garland and White (1980) studied nine nurseries in London; three public sector and six private sector. The research consisted of a series of descriptive case studies of the functioning of the nurseries at the level of overall organisation and at the level of childcare, with little quantitative data. Organisational factors such as the ideology of adult-child relationships influenced childcare practices. While all nurseries had staff who worked long hours for poor pay and with generally short job tenure, there were also some marked differences between public and private sector provision. Private sector nurseries had staff with lower levels of training and qualifications and also a markedly worse staff:child ratio.

Other studies of nurseries have focused on public sector nurseries. While the results of these studies are useful in describing the characteristics of the children, staff and organisation of these institutions, they do not lend themselves to generalisation about nursery care, due to the highly selective group of children admitted to local authority nurseries. Bain and Barnett (1980) studied twelve children at one Social Service

Department nursery in London. The majority of the children had problematic home backgrounds, and Bain and Barnett concluded that the nursery experience added to children's developmental difficulties and that these became apparent at school; but without adequate comparison groups these conclusions could be misleading. The study did reveal issues of concern including the high number of caretakers for the children and consequent instability of care, the youth and inexperience of the staff and the high level of aggression in the nursery.

Some studies have revealed a high level of problem behaviours exhibited by children in Social Services day nurseries (McGuire and Richman 1986). Part of the reason for this high occurrence is the priorities applied in determining admission to the small number of public day nurseries; these priorities ensure that most children come from disturbed or disadvantaged backgrounds, have handicapping conditions or are otherwise deemed to be 'at risk'. Young children, however, show rapid learning of behaviours from their peers, and hence it may well be that a problem behaviour initially exhibited by one child in a nursery will be learnt by others, so rapidly increasing the incidence of such behaviours. To the extent that this process occurs, such nurseries may function as training schools in problem behaviours.

Staff in Social Services nurseries do not have special training for coping with problem behaviours yet they encounter such behaviours to a greater degree than staff in other nurseries. Could extra staff training help? Could organizational change in such nurseries help? These are questions that are open to empirical enquiry and the answers would aid practitioners. It would seem likely that greater integration of pre-school children from at risk populations with children from the general population would be helpful, but this would require a change either in the admission policies of Social Services nurseries or a new strategy for the day care of such children.

Another study by McGuire and Richman (1988) drew attention to the linkages between management style, group structure and child behaviour in six Social Services nurseries. The study relied on interviews with nursery staff and systematic observations of children in the nurseries. Using data from their analysis of interviews with staff, McGuire and Richman describe a dimension of management style, which they term 'ethos', which varied from an autocratic, rigid adult-centred approach to a more democratic, flexible, child-centred approach. The more autocratic management styles were associated with larger group size. Where the head of the nursery was more openly involved with staff and children, there was greater parental consultation and more adult initiated interaction with children.

The management style therefore had an effect on the nature of children's interactions and of parent-worker relationships, and emphasises again how features of the day care environment can affect the experience of children (and parents).

The TCRU Day Care Project

The largest and most recent British day care research has been a longitudinal study of 255 two parent families having a first child. In the main part of the sample, the mother resumed full-time employment after maternity leave. Children in these dual-earner households were admitted to full-time day care before the age of 9 months and were divided into three sub-groups according to the type of care used – childminders, nurseries or relatives. In a fourth sub-group of the sample, the mother did not resume employment after maternity leave. Mothers and children have been seen on 4 occasions – at 5, 18, 36 and 72 months after the birth, with mothers only being seen at 11 months, Caregivers were also visited when the child was 18 and 36 months of age. A wide range of methods have been used to collect data on parents, children and caregivers, including interviews, developmental assessments, observations and various schedules completed by the mothers (for further details of the design of the study and of the sample, see Melhuish 1990, Brannen and Moss 1990).

Data collection began in 1982 and finished in Spring 1990. This paper concentrates on the contacts up to 36 months, and on the child data (for fuller accounts of the mothers' experience, see Brannen and Moss 1988, 1990). During this three year stage, the study had a very low attrition rate, losing only 12 of the original 255 households.

The day care settings

Children in dual-earner households were divided between three types of day care – childminders, relatives and nurseries. The nursery children proved the hardest sub-group to find. At the beginning of the study in 1982/3, we looked for nurseries which would take children under 12 months of age from two parent families where both parents were employed full-time. These criteria ruled out local authority day nurseries and left very few other nurseries. In the whole Greater London area we found only 33 nurseries taking this young age group of babies. Only 3 were for-profit nurseries. Most were workplace-attached, all of them providing for public sector employees; hospital creches were the most common. In practice, therefore, the very limited nursery provision in London was mostly available only to a small number of parents working for a few employers. Nurseries were not an option for most parents, though amongst those who eventually used childminders a quarter said they would have preferred a nursery (and another quarter said they would have preferred a nanny).

The eventual nursery sub-group of children was distributed between 18 nurseries, and in these cases observations were made in the nurseries of the activities and interactions of these children from the sample. Interviews were conducted with the officers-in-charge of these nurseries, and of all but two of the remaining 15 nurseries. From these interviews, the basic characteristics of these nurseries emerged. Accommodation was varied. Two nurseries were purpose-built and the rest were housed in converted buildings where the conversions ranged from minimal to extensive. Staff complained about accommodation in over half of the nurseries, the most common complaint concerning insufficient space. The number of children varied from 12 to 50, although one centre, which combined a nursery and nursery school, had 88 children. There was always a high demand for places, particularly for babies. Eighty per cent of the staff had a childcare qualification, but only 31 per cent had their own children. Staff pay and working conditions were often poor.

It was noticeable that a number of the nurseries were under-resourced. This was reflected in poor levels of staffing, discussed below, and in the poor pay and conditions and poor accommodation, already referred to, that occurred in some nurseries. This under-resourcing was a consequence of parents who used the nurseries not being highly paid (for example, teachers, nurses and other health service workers) and employers who lacked the means or commitment to provide substantial levels of subsidy.

The nurseries were also extremely isolated. They were either entirely independent or else marginal parts of large organisations. Nine were not registered with local authorities, because they were in hospitals, and only 12 reported regular visits either from Social Services Departments or from any other public health or welfare agency. It should be added that childminders in the study also received relatively little support. Nearly half the childminders said they had not been visited by a local authority worker in the preceding 6 months, only a quarter had ever started a training course, 15 per cent currently used a toy library and just one out of over 60 went to a childminders' group.

I have described the nurseries at some length and the unsatisfactory circumstances in which a number of them operated. In view of some of the subsequent results from this study, it is important to do so, and to emphasise that the results relate specifically to this group of nurseries, operating in the circumstances just described. Table 1 provides some comparison between features of the nursery provision and the other types of day care studied. It is noticeable how the adult:child ratios vary between nurseries, but in general are worst in nurseries and best with relatives. Moreover the nursery figure overestimates the number of adults actually involved with children, as it does not allow for staff absence through illness, other duties or leave. During the observations of the children conducted at the 18 month contact, the actual adult:child ratios for nurseries were often worse than Table 1 indicates.

Table 1

Characteristics of Day Care Settings

	Relative	C/Minder	Nursery	
Mean group size	1.3	2.5	7.5	27
Range	1–3	1–5	6–12	12–50
Mean child:adult	1.3	2.5	4.6	
Range	1–3	1–5	2.4–8.5	
Mean age c/g	51	38	31	
Range	27–62	26–55	18–57	
Mean cost £/week 1984/1985	11	27	34	
Per cent with childcare qualification	0	14	80	
Per cent c/gs mothers	100	98	31	

All the children in the three day care sub-groups entered day care before the age of 9 months and experienced, on average, 20 months of day care during their first 3 years. While in day care, nearly half the children had at least one change of placement. Placements in nurseries were least likely to end in a move, although children in nurseries would have experienced some changes in nursery workers due to staff turnover. Changes in childminder and relative placements were almost twice as common. For example, 42 per cent of childminder placements ended in a move, over half because the parents, children or childminders were unhappy with the arrangement, or because the childminder stopped childminding.

Since the study there have been some changes in the day care situation. Between 1985 and 1988, the numbers of private nurseries in London increased by more than 60 per cent, and the pace of change may have quickened subsequently. Private provision is undoubtedly continuing to grow, some of it workplace-attached, with private sector employers now taking the lead, but mostly for profit nurseries, a type of provision that was not common in the early 1980's, at least for babies.

However, we do not know how many of the new private nurseries take children under 2, anything about their quality, what parents pay for a place or anything about their cost structure, for example the pay and conditions of their workers; in other words, it is not possible to say whether a sample of current nurseries admitting children under 12 months would produce significantly different results and reveal significantly better conditions.

The children at
5 months

The first contact of the study was timed for 4–5 months after the birth, just before most of the mothers in the sample had resumed employment. Comparisons between the four groups of children could therefore be made before most of them had had any experience of day care. At this stage, there were no differences either of developmental status or temperament, while observations of mother-infant interactions revealed that there were no overall differences between the four sub-groups in patterns of mother- infant interactions.

There was however an unexpected interaction effect with child gender. In the sub-group of women who were not to return to employment, mothers tended to exhibit more interaction with boys than girls. This gender difference did not emerge for women who would return to employment. Such an effect may reflect greater gender equality in dual-earner households. The other main difference within the sample emerged from diaries that the mothers kept of one week of the child's activities. These diary records showed that children who would enter day care full-time were experiencing more babysitting even before the mothers resumed employment. This probably reflected the need for women to resolve outstanding domestic business before the return to employment and hence needing some time free of child care responsibilities, as well as possibly an element of accustoming children to non-parental care.

The children at
18 months

When the children were 18 months, the child's main daytime caregiver was contacted and interviewed, child-caregiver interactions were observed, children's development was assessed and mothers were interviewed. The focal observations of the children at 18 months with their main daytime caregiver have been described in detail elsewhere (Melhuish, Mooney, Martin and Lloyd, 1990). A study child was observed for an hour of free play on two days. The child's behaviour and others' behaviour directed to the child were recorded in a continuous sequence, which allowed the sequence of behaviour as well as the amount of different behaviours to be studied.

A number of differences emerged in the characteristics of the interactions of children in the different caregiving environments. The interactional behaviours which differed across settings included attention to the child, attention by the child to others, group activities, affection to the child, verbal and non-verbal communications to the child and from the child, and responsiveness to the child's communications. In the literature of adult-child interactions, the importance of affection, communication and responsiveness have consistently been emphasised (for example, by Ainsworth, Blehar, Waters and Wall 1978, Clarke-Stewart 1973). Similar attributes, particularly communication and responsiveness, are included as key elements in measures of the quality of day care environments (for example, Harms and Clifford 1980).

In our observations of children and their caregivers, similar patterns emerged for each of these three key aspects of affection, communications and responsiveness. The children cared for at home and by relatives had higher scores (in other words, their caregivers showed more affection, communication and responsiveness) than the childminder sub-group, which was in turn higher than the nursery sub-group. The home and relative sub-groups were in situations where a child was with a family member (either its mother or a relative) and hence the differences in affection might be expected due to the nature of the emotional bond between caregiver and child. The differences in other behaviours, including communication and responsiveness, probably reflect the effects of adult:child ratio and group size (since at that stage in the study, most mothers and relatives had only one child to care for).

Previous studies of parent-child interaction (Clarke-Stewart 1973) and children in day care (McCartney 1984) have found associations between differences in communication and responsiveness and language development. This was also the case in the TCRU Day Care Project. At eighteen months of age, various aspects of the children's development were measured (for a full description of the results, see Melhuish et al. 1990, Melhuish 1987). There was no evidence of day care effects in *cognitive development* as measured by a standardized developmental assessment. *Language development* was measured by each mother keeping a record of all of her child's utterances during the course of one week. These records gave the child's productive language capacity in terms of number of single words and number of word combinations. The differences between day care groups were not significant for the number of single words. There were however significant differences related to the number of word combinations, with the children in the nursery sub-group being less likely than the other sub-groups to have high scores for word combinations.

This difference (and any others reported in this paper) emerged after allowing for the effects of developmental status at the start of the study, mother's education and child gender in a logistic regression analysis. However when two variables derived from the child-caregiver observations – 'communications received by child' and 'responsiveness to child's communications' – were also put into this regression analysis, the effect for nursery care disappeared. It would appear therefore that the difference for the nursery sub-group was a result of the different pattern of interactions occurring in the nurseries, particularly in terms of communications and responsiveness received by the child – in other words, that the difference in language is not due to type of care per se but to specific features of adult-child interaction in the examples of that type of care under study. This would suggest that if the nurseries in our sample had had higher levels of communication and responsiveness such results would not have occurred.

The *socio-emotional development* of the children at 18 months of age was measured by three techniques, two of which were based on an observer's report, while one was based on mothers' reports:

1. A stranger approach/separation/reunion sequence was followed during a home visit. There was a set approach sequence for the female stranger (the researcher) towards the child. During this approach, positive and negative signs of emotional response by the child to the stranger were noted. After this approach, the mother left the room and the child's reaction upon being separated from the mother were noted. After two minutes of separation, the mother entered the room and the child's response upon reunion was noted.

2. Seven ratings were completed by the observer after the home visit. These ratings were responsiveness to persons, mother and observer, co-operativeness, fearfulness, tension and general emotional tone.

3. A socio-emotional development questionnaire was completed by mothers. This questionnaire focused on the child's actual behaviour rather than parental attitudes, and was developed by the T C R U research team because no equivalent method existed for 18 month old children. The questionnaire covered sociability, emotional expression, self punishing behaviours, empathy, fear of stranger, separation anxiety, tolerance of departures from daily routine, and independence.

In the stranger approach sequence, children in the nursery sub-group showed less positive responses to the stranger than the other children, but did not differ in negative responses. It appeared therefore that nursery children were less excited by a stranger than the other children in the study, probably due to their greater experience of unfamiliar adults, and were no more fearful of a stranger. Upon separation from the mother, the children in the sub-group cared for by their mothers at home during the day seemed to be the least upset, followed by the relative and childminder sub-groups with the nursery sub-group most likely to be upset. In view of the 'Belsky' debate, could this reflect differences in attachment? Probably not: response upon reunion is the most significant indicator in assessing attachment and this showed no difference between the subgroups.

The Infant Behaviour Record also pointed to different socio-emotional behaviour for the nursery children. On the basis of their behaviour during the home visit, they were rated by the researchers as showing less orientation to people and more negative mood, which is consistent with the results of the approach/separation/reunion sequence. By contrast, the questionnaire completed by mothers did not reveal any differences associated with day care. This discrepancy with the results from the two other assessments, which were based upon the researchers' reports, may reflect the differing frame of reference for mothers, who mostly would have less experience of similar age children, and also perhaps a tendency to idealise the behaviour of their own child.

The children at 36 months

The next stage of the study occurred when the children were 3 years old, when a similar range of data were collected from child, mother and caregiver. The interview data with the caregivers revealed a similar picture to that which had existed 18 months earlier in terms of the basic characteristics of caregivers and the caregiving environment. The observations of the children in the main caregiving environment followed the same course as at 18 months, except that the range of behaviours recorded had been altered to reflect the different behaviourial repertoires of 3 year olds.

Substantial differences were again observed in the interactions which occurred in the different care settings; these probably reflect the same differences as at the 18 months contact in caregiving environments for variables such as group size and adult:child ratios. The amount of verbal communication from the child, group play and peer play and peer interactions had all increased since the previous contact. The nursery children showed more group and peer play than the other children, as a result of the greater opportunities available to them for these activities. The pattern of results for affection to the child, communications and responsiveness all showed a similar pattern of results to 18 months earlier, with the highest levels among the home and relative sub-groups followed by the childminder sub-group and the lowest levels among the nursery sub-group. The difference in communications applied whether total, verbal or non-verbal were considered and the differences in responsiveness held for all communications from the child, responses to child questions or responses to child commands. These differences were still apparent despite the increase in peer interactions which had occurred, particularly in nurseries, and which contributed to the results.

The cognitive and linguistic development of the children at 3 years of age was measured by two non-verbal and two verbal sub-scales of the British Ability Scales. These sub-scales were visual recognition, digit span, naming vocabulary and verbal comprehension, and they could be combined together to give an overall I Q. For this overall measure of I Q there were no day care effects. However when the sub-scales were considered separately, there was a tendency for the nursery sub-group to have fewer children scoring highly on the naming vocabulary sub-test (having controlled, again, for initial developmental status, mother's education and child gender). This result implies that the earlier difference in language development found at 18 months of age was persisting at 3 years of age.

The socio-emotional development of the children at 3 years old was again measured using three techniques:

1. The Behavioural Screening Questionnaire (Richman and Graham 1971) was completed by the mother, and focuses on behaviour problems.

2. A Social Behaviour Questionnaire was adapted by the research team from an earlier questionnaire used in a study of Project Headstart in the U S A . This questionnaire gave scores for the child on aggression, verbal sociability, independence, timidity and positive sociability, and was completed by the mother.

3. Following a home visit, the researchers' rated children for responsiveness to persons, mother and observer, co-operativeness, fearfulness, tension and general emotional tone, in the same way as they had done at the 18 months contact.

There was less timidity and more sociability and talking to the observer, cooperation and positive mood, the greater the amount of day care experienced over the child's first three years of life. The effects were stronger when the amount of day care for the period 18 to 36 months was considered, suggesting that recent day care experience is most important in influencing social behaviour. There was also one significant effect on socio-emotional development associated with type of day care (as opposed to total amount of any kind of day care). Children in the nursery sub-group showed higher levels of positive sociability, i.e. behaviours such as sharing, co-operation and empathy, than other children, suggesting a positive effect of nursery experience.

Conclusion

The results from the TCRU Day Care Project show no evidence of negative results from early full-time day care or from the total amount of day care experienced in the first three years. Because the study did not use the 'Strange Situation' technique, which is the standard measure of attachment in young children, the results cannot make a direct contribution to the 'Belsky debate'; we cannot say whether or not the children in our sample admitted to full-time day care under 12 months of age were more likely to have an insecure attachment to their mothers at 18 or 36 months, though there is no hint of this from our indirect evidence. The 6 year contact will however address this isue directly, as it is collecting data on attachment and on the types of behaviour that it is argued are a consequence of insecure attachment.

The study however does show some 'type of day care' effects, negative with respect to aspects of language and positive with respect to aspects of socio-emotional development. Do the negative results mean that nursery care is not advisable for children under 3? The answer is almost certainly no. The effects on language development among nursery children in the study are most appropriately interpreted as reflecting features of the care provided in the nurseries studied, or at least some of them, and not as inherent consequences of nursery care per se. The nature of the child's interactional experience was the main predictor of language development and in this study this was closely related to type of care; type of care was therefore confounded by type of interaction.

This interpretation is supported by Swedish research reported in the chapter by Philip Hwang, which find no evidence of differential negative effects for nursery care. A number of American studies (Carew 1980, Rubenstein and Howes 1983, McCartney 1984) report that children enrolled in day care facilities with more responsive caregivers had high language development scores.

The important issue for policy therefore is not so much whether children should be in one type of day care or another, but that whatever type they are in provides enhancing experience and particularly positive interactions between adults and children. A number of conditions appear to facilitate this type of environment. Group size was found to be important for adult-child interactions by Ruopp, Travers, Glantz and Coelen (1979) and similar results are reported in experimental groups studied by Schaffer and Liddell (1984). Adult:child ratio, which is associated with group size, has also been found to have an effect (Sylva et al. 1980, Howes 1990). Stability of caregivers, related to staff turnover, was associated with language and social development of children in the National Day Care Staffing Study (Whitebook et al. 1989), with poor pay and conditions strongly related to high turnover. The demands other than childcare made on staff are likely to affect the quantity and quality of staff-child interaction. Finally, aspects of child-adult interaction may be amenable to improvement through good training programmes and other forms of support; sensitive responsiveness, for example, could be enhanced with the help of these kinds of intervention.

All these conditions which are likely to facilitate good adult-child interactions in nurseries (or any other kind of day care setting) are unlikely to be found in poorly resourced services or in isolated day care settings. The results from the Day Care Project, and other research, point strongly to the central importance of the social context, which determines the resources and support systems available to day care workers and the types of day care experience available to young children.

References

Ainsworth, M. D. S., Blehar, M. L., Waters, E. and Wall, S. (1978). *Patterns of attachment: A psychological study of the strange situation*. Hillsdale, N.J.: Lawrence Erlbaum Associates.

Bain, A. & Barnett, L. (1980). *The design of a day care system in a nursery setting for children under five*. Report to the Department of Health and Social Security.

Brannen, J. & Moss, P. (1988). *New mothers at work*. London: Unwin Hyman.

Brannen, J. & Moss, P. (1990). *Managing mothers: Dual-earner households in early parenthood*. London: Unwin Hyman

Bryant, B., Harris, M. & Newton, D. (1980). *Children and Minders*. London: Grant McIntyre.

Carew, J.V. (1980). *Experience and development of intelligence in young children at home and in day care*. Monographs of the Society for Research in Child Development, 45 (6–7, Serial No. 187).

Clarke-Stewart, K. A. (1973). *Interactions between mothers and their young children*. Monographs of the Society for Research in Child Development, *38*, (6–7, Serial No. 153).

Davie, C. (1986). *An investigation into childminding in North Staffordshire*. Report to the Department of Health and Social Security.

Garland, C. & White, S. (1980). *Children and day nurseries*. London: Grant McIntyre.

Harms, T. & Clifford, R. (1980). *Early childhood environment rating scale*. New York: Teacher's College Press, Columbia University.

Howes, C. (1990). 'Caregiving environment for young children: The experience in the United States'. In E. C. Melhuish & P. Moss (eds.) *Day care for young Children: International Perspectives*. London: Routledge.

McCartney, K. (1984). 'Effects of quality of day care environment on children's language development'. *Developmental Psychology, 20*, 244–260.

McGuire, J. & Richman, N. (1986). 'Screening for behaviour problems in nurseries'. *Journal of Child Psychology and Psychiatry, 27*, 7–32.

McGuire, J. & Richman, N. (1988). *Institutional characteristics and staff behaviour*. Paper presented to the Annual Conference of the British Psychological Society, Leeds, April, 1988.

Mayall, B. & Petrie, P. (1977). *Minder, mother and child.* London: University of London Institute of Education.

Melhuish, E. C. (1987). 'Socio-emotional behaviour at 18 months as a function of day care experience, temperament and gender'. *Infant Mental Health Journal, 8,* 364–373.

Melhuish, E. C. (1990). 'Research on day care for young children in the United Kingdom'. In E. C. Melhuish and P. Moss (eds.) *Day care for young children: International perspectives.* London: Routledge.

Melhuish, E. C., Mooney, A., Martin, S. & Lloyd, E. (1990). 'Type of day care at 18 months: I Differences in interactional experience'. *Journal of Child Psychology and Psychiatry, 31,* 849–859.

Melhuish, E. C., Lloyd, E., Martin, S. & Mooney, A. (1990). 'Type of day care at 18 months: II Relations with cognitive and language development'. *Journal of Child Psychology and Psychiatry, 31,* 860–870.

Moore, T. W. (1975). 'Exclusive early mothering and its alternatives: The outcome to adolescence'. *Scandinavian Journal of Psychology 16,* 255–272.

Moss, P. (1987). *A review of childminding research.* Thomas Coram Research Unit Occasional and Working paper No. 6. London: Institute of Education.

Raven, M. (1981). 'Review: The effects of childminding: How much do we know?' *Child: Care, Health and Development, 7,* 103–111.

Richman, N. and Graham, P. (1971). 'A behavioural screening questionnaire for three year olds'. *Journal of Child Psychology and Psychiatry, 12,* 5–33.

Rubenstein, J. L., and Howes, C. (1983). 'Socio-emotional development of toddlers in day care: The role of peers and individual differences'. In S. Kilmer (ed.) *Advances in Early Education and Day Care.* San Francisco: J A I Press.

Ruopp, R., Travers, J., Glantz, F. & Coelen, C. (1979). *Children at the center: Final results of the national day care study.* Cambridge, MA: Abt Associates.

Schaffer, H. R. & Liddell, C. (1984). 'Adult-child interaction under dyadic and polyadic conditions'. *British Journal of Developmental Psychology, 2,* 33–42.

Shinman, S. (1981). *A choice for every child? Access and response to pre-school provision.* London: Tavistock.

Sylva, K., Roy, C. and Painter, H. (1980). *Childwatching at Playgroup and Nursery School.* London: Grant McIntyre.

Whitebook, M., Howes, C. & Phillips, D. (1989). *The National Child Care Staffing Study.* Oakland: Child Care Employee Project.

Educational Aspects of Day Care in England and Wales

Kathy Sylva

The effects of pre-school experience

Children most at risk for a poor start to school are those from disadvantaged homes (Mortimore and Blackstone 1982) and/or those who attend Social Services day nurseries (Osborn and Milbank 1987). This leads to a dilemma: the interest of national welfare and individual families is prompting women into work, but more women in the workforce will require more day care services. What are day care children like, and how do they fare when they 'graduate' to primary school and beyond? Douglas (1990) paints a graphic picture:

> 'The present structure of providing pre-school day care provision leads to differences in the prevalence of behaviour problems in different pre-school settings (McGuire and Richman 1986). Day nurseries now offer provision mostly to children from homes where child abuse, inadequate parenting or poor home conditions indicate a necessity for alternate day time care to be provided for the child. They cope with four times as many behaviour problems in the children as those in nursery schools and ten times as many as those in playgroups. The most difficult behaviours include anti-social behaviour, aggression, conduct disorders and poor attention. Altogether 56 per cent of the day nursery children have a speech, health, developmental or behavioural problem indicating the great stress and complexity of problems that staff face in these settings'.

This is worrying on its own, of course, but also worrying because children with the kind of behaviour problems described by Douglas go on to become poor readers (Richman, Stevenson and Graham 1982). Furthermore, the Osborn and Milbank study of a much larger sample of children found that attendance at day nursery (primarily social services nurseries) was associated with anti-social behaviour and poor reading scores at age ten. Should we abolish day care?

What research has actually shown us is not that day care causes difficulties in development; rather it alerts us to the fact that the kinds of children who attend Social Services day care are more likely to experience developmental problems than children who attend other, or no provision. The large survey by Osborn and Milbank found that children from 'home playgroups' did best and children from Social Services nurseries worst in comparisons of educational achievement at age ten. However in Britain the home backgrounds of children affect the likelihood of using different types of pre-school services very markedly (e.g. admission to Social Services nurseries is largely determined by disadvantaged home background and 'home playgroups' are largely used by children from advantaged homes). Where such marked covariance of variables occurs, the methodological difficulties of adequately controlling for home background factors can be immense, hence such findings should be interpreted cautiously (see Woodhead 1989 for a fuller discussion).

There is evidence to show that preschool experience can be a 'plus' in children's lives. Overall the evidence for the beneficial effects of pre-school experience for three-to-five year olds on later educational achievement and social adjustment appears to be strong, but the quality of provision will be vital.

There has been extensive research in the USA on the possible benefits of pre-school experience for disadvantaged children's later development. This research has largely focussed on compensatory pre-school programmes, such as Project Headstart, which were part of a 'War on Poverty'. This research has had a controversial history with initially favourable results being followed by claims that the effects were temporary. Then with later evidence, it turned out that there were measureable long-term beneficial effects (e.g. Lazar et al 1982). Beneficial effects from pre-school education have also been found in India (Sharma 1987) and in other developing countries such as Chile (Halpern and Myers 1985), showing that early childhood experiences are worthwhile in a variety of cultures.

No doubt the controversy over research designs will continue. However, at the moment the evidence suggests that preschool experience can have long-term benefits, not only for social and educational development, but also in economic terms. The recipients of high quality pre-school education programs have shown a wide range of favourable personal, social and educational outcomes such as less criminal behaviour, less dependence on social welfare and less need for remedial education throughout their childhood and youth. The later research has shown that the most marked effects are not limited to intellectual or educational outcomes; Table 1 summarizes the main findings on 123 disadvantaged children who had attended the High/Scope preschool programme in the USA. While not all pre-school provision will lead to such startling results

(Woodhead 1985), the High/Scope study shows that it can. A cost-benefit analysis comparing the costs of providing pre-school education with the costs of the increased crime, social welfare reliance and remedial education etc. which would occur without pre-school education, suggests that preschool education is a good bet in economic terms (Berrueta-Clement et al 1984).

Table 1

Major findings at age 19 in the Perry Pre-school (High/Scope) study

	Group		
Outcome	Attended pre-school	Did not attend pre-school	p Value
% Employed (n=121)	59	32	0.032
% High school graduate (or its equivalent) (n=121)	67	49	0.034
% With college or vocational training (n=121)	38	21	0.029
% Ever detained or arrested (n=121)	31	51	0.022
Females only: teen pregnancies/100 (n=49)	64	117	0.084
Functional competence (APL survey: possible score 40) (n=109)	24.6	21.8	0.025
% Of years in special education (n=112)	16	28	0.039

Source: Beruetta-Clement et al, 1986

There is also British evidence of the benefits for the later educational attainment of children who have pre-school experience. Osborn and Milbank (1987) used data from a national sample to look at the relationship between pre-school experience and educational achievement at ten years of age, after allowing for home background. They found that most pre-school experiences were associated with better educational achievement and that such effects were apparently not limited to children from disadvantaged homes. This large-scale research is also supported by some small-scale studies; for example, Turner (1977) found that, for children from similar home backgrounds, those that had attended playgroups showed benefits in social and intellectual development over those without pre-school experience.

At first sight it might appear that pre-school experience has its effects by giving an initial boost to children. While there is some truth in this, it is too simple an explanation. The effects are probably mediated largely through a complex process involving how the child and educators relate, how the child's family relates to education, educators and the community, and how the child and family come to view their child's capabilities. The pre-school experience may be the gateway to a succession of mutually supportive factors contributing to the child's progress.

A curriculum for the 3–5's: Quality in education

Which pre-school experiences will lead to a 'good start' at school? The HMI Report 'Aspects of Primary Education: The Education of Children Under Five' (Department of Education and Science 1989) stated clearly that general principles pertaining to the planning and monitoring of the primary curriculum also applied to the education of children 3–5. Children at this age learn through structured play and exploration, experiences which can be stimulated and guided by adults. However, an effective play curriculum requires individualised assessment of all aspects of children's development. Structured play and developmental assessment are the twin foundations upon which the National Curriculum will rest.

The concern here is that children in day care may not receive an adequate programme of guided play to put them firmly on the first rung of the National Curriculum. There is a great need to establish higher quality day care, be it centre- or home-based, with strong educational input. Staff in day nurseries have been shown to be less educational in their orientation than staff in school-based provision; unfortunately the advent of the National Curriculum could seriously disadvantage children in day nurseries and childminding. It has been argued that the day care side to pre-school provision requires a stronger educational input (House of Commons, 1989) whereas reception class provision needs a less formal approach to early schooling (Pascal and Ghaye, 1988).

It is important to re-address and build upon the recommendations concerning the quality of educational experiences offered to three and four year olds which were set out in the Select Committee Report on Achievement the Under-Fives (House of Commons 1989), in particular the recommendations in this Report relating to the upgrading of staffing levels, post-experience training, resources and curriculum arrangements for children in day care.

The debate about education in day care settings has drawn attention to contradictions in curriculum for children under fives. There is some confusion amongst nursery nurses and teachers about the appropriateness of various curriculum models for planning and implementating the curriculum. Different beliefs and practices emanating from past policies and ideologies in early years educational and childcare provision include:

(a) The British nursery school tradition of structured play provision and practical group or individual activities such as baking, sand and water play, craftwork and table top games.

(b) The Elementary School tradition with an emphasis on the basic skills of literacy and numeracy.

(c)   The USA tradition of a 'cognitively orientated' curriculum, such as High/Scope.

(d)   The Developmental Curriculum based on the freedom of the individual child to learn through self-chosen active learning activities.

(e)   The Thematic Based approach to curriculum planning derived from Primary School practice.

(f)   The Health and Care Orientated tradition of day care provision with an emphasis on the physical and social well-being of the child.

Until now, there has been happy agreement in both the state and voluntary sectors in favour of (a) and (d), with (e) appearing sometimes in infant schools. Children are likely to meet any one or a mixture of these models before they are filtered into the National Curriculum at five. The diversity of their educational experiences will be further exacerbated by the wide variations and inequalities in their access to pre-five education. There is a need to clarify the aims and approaches which characterise good practice in a curriculum for early years education so that we do not end up with one curriculum in the 'care' sector and another in the 'education' sector. The education sector may be moving towards (c) and (e) while the care sector remains focussed on (a) and (d).

The National Curriculum and children under five

Wherever they work, teachers and carers of children under five should be aware of the programmes of study and attainment targets of Key Stage 1 (DES 1990b, 1990c). Many of the attainment targets at Level 1 are well within the range of achievement of many four year olds and some three year olds. Tables 2 and 3 show levels and statements of attainment in two Maths attainment targets. Tables 3 and 4 show levels and statements of attainment in two Science attainment targets. Recall that most children in Key Stage One (5–7 years) will be operating somewhere in the range which includes levels 1–3. But many children are capable of level 1 skill and/or knowledge before they enter school, while others will work towards it after entry into formal schooling. What is important is that pre-school workers – no matter where they work – know about the National Curriculum and methods for assessing children's progress. The Early Years Curriculum Group (1989) has produced a thoughtful guide to early years activities and planning, all based on the National Curriculum.

Table 2 *Attainment Target 2: Number*

Pupils should understand number and number notation.

Level	Statements of attainment	Example
	Pupils should:	
1	•count, read, write and order numbers to at least 10; know that the size of a set is given by the last number in the count.	
	•understand the conservation of number.	Know that if a set of 8 pencils is counted, the answer is always the same however they are arranged.
2	•read, write and order numbers to at least 100; use the knowledge that the tens-digit indicates the number of tens.	Know that 37 means 3 tens and 7 units; know that three 10p coins and four 1p coins give 34p.
	•understand the meaning of 'a half' and 'a quarter'.	Find a quarter of a piece of string; know that half of 8 is 4.
3	•read, write and order numbers to at least 1000; use the knowledge that the position of a digit indicates its value.	Know that 'four hundred and two's is written 402 and why neither 42 nor 4002 is correct.
	•use decimal notation as the conventional way of recording in money.	Know that three £1 coins plus six 1p coins is written as £3.06, and that 3–6 on a calculator means £3.60 in the context of money.
	•appreciate the meaning of negative whole numbers in familiar contexts.	Read a temperature scale; understand a negative output on a calculator.
4	•read, write and order whole numbers.	
	•understand the effect of multiplying a whole number by 10 or 100.	Explain why the cost of 10 objects costing £23 each is £230.
	•use, with understanding, decimal notation to two decimal places in the context of measurement.	Read scales marked in hundredths and numbered in tenths (1.89m).
	•recognise and understand simple everyday fractions.	Estimate ⅓ of milk or ¾ of the length of a piece of wood.
	•recognise and understand simple percentages.	Know that 7 books out of a total of 100 books represents 7%.
	•understand and use of the relationship between place values in whole numbers.	Know that 5000 is 5 thousands or 50 hundreds or 500 tens or 5000 ones.

Table 3 *Attainment Target 9: Using and applying mathematics*

Pupils should use shape and space and handle data in practical tasks, in real-life problems, and to investigate within mathematics itself.

Level	Statements of attainment	Example
	Pupils should:	
1	•use materials provided for a task.	Make a collection of 3-D shapes from linking cubes.
	•talk about own work and ask questions.	Make up and tell stories about the 3-D shapes; ask questions such as: 'Which is the longest?'
	•make predictions based on experience.	Gain experience of the pattern of the school day; predict when the class will be in the hall for music and dance.
2	•select the materials and the mathematics to use for a task.	Sort and classify a collection of coloured plane shapes using own criteria.
	•describe current work, record findings and check results.	Describe how the classification of shapes was made and check the results.
	•ask and respond to the question: 'What would happen if...?'	Discuss a block graph showing the ways children in the class came to school that morning; respond to the question: 'How will the graph change if there are no buses running tomorrow?'
3	•select the materials and the mathematics to use for a task; check results and consider whether they are sensible.	Design and make a weather vane which involves reflective symmetry; test the weather vane and modify if necessary.
	•explain work being done and record findings systematically.	Keep a record of wind direction over a period of time; display the results in an appropriate chart and discuss the findings.
	•make and test publications.	Experiment with a collection of dice with different numbers of coloured faces; predict the outcomes of rolling each die 50 times and test the predictions.

Table 4 *Attainment target 2: The variety of life*

Pupils should develop their knowledge and understanding of the diversity and classification of past and present life-forms, and of the relationships, energy flows, cycles of matter and human influences within ecosystems.

Level	Statements of attainment
	Pupils should:
1	• know that there is a wide variety of living things, which includes human beings.
2	• know that plants and animals need certain conditions to sustain life.
	• understand how living things are looked after and be able to treat them with care and consideration.
3	• be able to recognise similarities and differences among living things.
	• be able to sort living things into broad groups according to observable features.
	• know that living things respond to seasonal and daily changes.
4	• be able to recognise similarities and differences both within and between groups of plants and animals.
	• understand the key factors in the process of decay (temperature, microbes, compactness, moisture) and how this is important in the re-use of biological material in everyday life.
	• understand that plants and animals can be preserved as fossils in different ways.
5	• understand that the differences in physical factors between localities, including differences in seasonal and daily changes, are reflected in the different species of plants and animals found there.
	• be able to assign organisms to their major groups using keys and observable features.
	• be able to support their view about environmental issues concerned with the use of fertilisers in agriculture and horticulture, based on their practical experience.
	• understand predator-prey relationships.

Table 5 *Attainment target 3: Process of life*

Pupils should develop their knowledge and understanding of the organisation of living things and of the processes which characterise their survival and reproduction.

Level	Statements of attainment
	Pupils should:
1	• be able to name or label the external parts of the human body/plants, for example, *arm, leg/flower, stem.*
2	• know that living things reproduce their own kind.
	• personal hygiene, food, exercise, rest and safety, and the proper and safe use of medicines are important.
	• be able to give a simple account of the pattern of their own day.
3	• know that the basic life processes: feeding, breathing, movement and behaviour, are common to human beings and the other living things they have studied.
	• be able to describe the main stages in the human life cycle.
4	• be able to name the major organs and organ systems in flowering plants, and mammals.
	• know about the factors which contribute to good health and body maintenance, including the defence systems of the body, balanced diet, oral hygiene and avoidance of harmful substances such as tobacco, alcohol and other drugs.
	• understand the process of reproduction in mammals.
	• be able to describe the main stages of flowering plant reproduction.
5	• know that living things are made up from different kinds of cells with carry out different jobs.
	• understand malnutrition and the relationships between diet, exercise, health, fitness and circulatory disorders.
	• know that in digestion food is made soluble so that it can enter the blood.
	• understand the way in which microbes and lifestyle affect health.
	• be able to describe the functions of the major organ systems.

The methods by which children should be encouraged towards developmental progress should be based on 'children's interests and appetite for play, building upon these to achieve educational objectives which complement, and have much in common with, the curriculum which they will receive in later years' (Department of Education and Science 1989a, para 65).

Many nursery teachers make detailed observations of children's progression in the broad areas of social, physical and intellectual development and in specific skill acquisition. This expertise will be valuable to colleagues in day nurseries to help them plan a curriculum which is in keeping with what lies ahead – the National Curriculum. Pupil profiles can inform day care staff about children's capabilities relating to the Key Stage 1 attainment targets. Profiles such as the Keele pre-school Assessment Guide (Tyler 1990) are useful in early years education/care, and may avoid demands by teachers for inappropriate 'baseline' testing of five year olds in order to establish 'entry points' to the National Curriculum. An effective pupil profile on all aspects of development, not just those in Key Stage One, seems an appropriate way of measuring where children 'are' in order to plan educational experiences for them.

Too formal – Too soon?
The educational sector is not without problems. Recent research has shown that many four year olds in reception classes are given tasks not tailored to their abilities (Bennett and Kell, 1989) and are assigned to ill equipped and poorly staffed classrooms (Pascal and Ghaye, 1988). Four year olds in reception classes are being taught by teachers trained for work with other children. Is their curriculum too formal? Research from abroad warns that early learning experiences which are too formal and school-like can lead to lower achievement later in school (Schweinhart et al., 1986). In fact there is a fierce outcry in the United States about the perils of 'too formal, too soon' approaches to early education (Zigler, 1987). It seems we are heading for two kinds of curriculum for children under five in England and Wales; the reception class where four year olds are given too formal a programme, and the day care sector where there is not enough carefully guided play and structured assessment.

A New, Multi-Professional Approach
What is required is a new, multi-professional approach to the early years. The care sector needs steady, informed input from teachers who are a regular part of the education-and-care team. The education sector needs more teachers trained to the particular needs of children under five and more resources for four year olds in reception classes. There needs to be greater

co-operation between local Education and Social Services departments so that a firm foundation is laid in day nurseries for the level 1 of each attainment target. The training of care-sector staff must take into account the National Curriculum. Similarly, the training of teachers must take into account the fact that they need skills for work outside the walls of the classroom. They must know how to co-ordinate their skills with those of other workers in the planning and monitoring of a curriculum based on structured play. They must have skill at inter-professional liaison with others concerned with the health and care of young children, for example social workers and health visitors. Co-ordination of this kind is the only way forward if we are not to have one pre-school curriculum for the poor and another for the better off.

References

Bennett, N. & Kell, J. (1989). *A Good Start? Four Year Olds in Infant Schools.* Oxford: Blackwell Education.

Berrueta-Clement J, Schweinhart, L. J., Barnett, W. S., Epstein, A. S., & Weikart, D. P. (1984). *Changed Lives: the effects of the Perry pre-school programme on youths through age 19.* Monographs of the High/Scope Educational Research Foundation 1984, No. 8.

Department of Education and Science (1989a). *Aspects of Primary Education: the education of children under five* (*HMI Report*) London: HMSO.

Department of Education and Science (1989b). *Mathematics in the National Curriculum.* London: HMSO.

Department of Education and Science (1989c). *Science in the National Curriculum.* London: HMSO.

Early Years Curriculum Group (1989). *Early Childhood Education. The Early Years Curriculum and the National Curriculum.* Trentham Books.

Douglas, J. (1990). 'Young children with behaviour problems'. *World Organization for Early Childhood Education UPDATE. No. 38,* 1–2.

Halpern, R. & Myers, R. (1985). *Effects of early childhood intervention on primary school progress and performance in the developing countries.* Unpublished paper. Ypsilanti, Mi: High/Scope – USAID.

House of Commons Committee on Education (1989). *Educational Provision for the Under Fives Vols. 1 & 2.* London, HMSO.

Lazar, I., Darlington, R. B., Murray, H. W. & Snipper, A. S. (1982). *Lasting effects of early education: a report from the Consortium for Longitudinal Studies.* Monographs of the Society for Research in Child Development, 47, Nos. 2–3.

Mortimore, J. & Blackstone, T. (1982). *Education and Disadvantage.* London: Heinemann.

Osborn, A. F. and Milbank, J. E. (1987). *The Effects of Early Education.* Oxford: Clarendon Press.

Pascal, C. & Ghaye, A. (1988). 'Four year old children in reception classrooms: participant perceptions and practice'. *Educational Studies Vol.14,* No. 2, 187–208.

Schweinhart, L. J., Weikart, D. P. & Larner, M. B. (1986). 'Consequences of three pre-school curriculum models through age 15'. *Early Childhood Research Quarterly, 1(1)*, 15–45.

Sharma, A. (1987). *Monitoring social components of integrated child development services*. New Delhi: National Institute of Public Co-operation and Child Development.

Turner, I. F. (1977). *Pre-school playgroup research and evaluation report*. Report submitted to the Department of Health and Social Security in Northern Ireland.

Tyler, S. (1990). *The Keele pre-school assessment guide (revised)*. Slough: NFER-Nelson.

Woodhead, M. (1985). 'Pre-school education has long term effects: but can they be generalized?' *Oxford Review of Education, 13,* 129–139.

Woodhead, M. (1989). 'Is early education effective?' In C. W. Desforges (ed.) *Early Childhood Education. British Journal of Educational Psychology Monograph Series 4.* Edinburgh: Scottish Academic Press.

Zigler, E. (1987). 'Formal schooling for four year olds? No'. *American Psychologist*, 254–260.

Future Directions for Day Care Policy and Research

Peter Moss and Edward Melhuish

Some lessons from research on day care

The chapters in this book provide a review of recent research on day care in three countries. A number of clear conclusions emerge:

1. There is no reason to believe that non-parental day care is inherently harmful, even for infants. The debate initiated by Jay Belsky in the United States is about whether or not full-time day care before 12 months may lead to an increased risk of certain adverse developments (though even in this debate it is not claimed that early full-time day care *inevitably* produces these effects). Alison Clarke-Stewart in her chapter also advises the need for caution in the development of infant day care, to identify more clearly under what circumstances infants in day care are likely to suffer. In view of the widespread existence of poor quality care in the United States revealed in the chapter by Alison Clarke-Stewart, it is quite possible that the adverse effects described by Belsky reflect the effects of poor quality care rather than non-parental care.

2. Assumptions are often made about the superiority of individual care (for example, by childminders) or group care (for example, in day nurseries). There is however no reason to believe that any of the main types of day care (childminders, relatives, nurseries) is inherently harmful. Given that parents show a range of preferences, there seems no need to be prescriptive. The issue again is to identify conditions in each setting which may increase the risk of adverse effects or increase the potential for positive effects.

Children are likely to benefit from an environment which provides a mixture of the best features from indivdual and group care. For example, good quality individual care can provide close attention to the individual needs of a child, while good quality group care can provide valuable social experience fostering social development: the balance needed between these qualities will vary between children, according to age, temperament and other factors. Individual attention can be enhanced in nursery settings where adequate staffing allows for some one-to-one interaction, as well as by other measures; while social experience can be enhanced in care by childminders, relatives or nannies where either other children are present or playgroups or drop-in centres are also used.

3. Day care effects will be mediated by the nature of the home environment, hence the importance of considering the total care environment of children. Home care varies from the abusive to the superb, and while the majority of parents provide good care for their children, factors such as depression, loneliness, marital disharmony and stress can affect anyone. The implications of the unavailability as well as the availability of different forms of care should be considered for the family as well as for the child.

4. Day care effects will also be mediated by children's experience in day care. The key issue is to identify what types of *experience* in day care enhance development, happiness and general well-being and what *conditions* are likely to encourage or discourage enhancing experiences (and also, of course, to identify what experiences may be harmful and what conditions foster these negative experiences). Here the research points to various types of positive experience, for example adult-child interactions characterised by affection, communication and sensitive responsivity; and to a range of ennabling conditions, for example a well organised and stimulating physical environment, a balanced curriculum, small group size and sufficient adult:child ratios, staff stability and, related to this last point, training, pay and conditions appropriate to the demands and skill required of the work.

The details of these conditions may vary with circumstances, for example infants require different levels of staffing and group size. More work is also needed to identify other conditions and refine our understanding of optimal conditions. Developmental or other outcomes do not necessarily keep on improving as conditions improve; the relationship in many cases is curvilinear. Moreover, while the right conditions may be necessary to provide enhancing experiences and good outcomes, they do not guarantee them. Continuous work is needed to monitor quality and provide support where problems occur.

The concept of quality

Services which provide experiences that enhance children's development may be considered to provide good quality care. Such a statement, while it may appear unproblematic at first sight, begs a number of questions. Human development spans a broad range of areas – intellectual, social, emotional, physical, aesthetic, moral and so on. In some areas, there may be disagreement about what types of development are desirable, while others may disagree about the priorities to be given as

132

between different areas of development. Similar problems occur in attempts to define quality in terms of some concept of children's rights – again, there are likely to be disagreements about what rights children have, prioritising rights and defining them. In both cases, we face the issue that defining quality is essentially a value-based operation. By its nature, it cannot be value-free nor can it be determined solely by researchers. The role of researchers is to provide ideas and information which can assist in achieving quality, once that concept is defined.

The issue of quality also goes beyond quality of *care*. This might be considered one component, albeit a vital one, in a wider concept of quality of *service*. This broader concept might need to encompass the impact of day care provision on groups other than children – mothers, fathers, workers, the local community and so on.

Finally, an even broader concept involves the quality of *service system*. The focus here is on the overall set of services serving a local community, a local authority or even the whole country. Some countries, such as the United States, have centres of excellence in services which provide high quality care to children and a high quality *service;* but the quality of the overall *system,* in the country as a whole, seems at best mediocre. On this criteria of quality of service system, other countries, such as Sweden and Denmark, would appear to perform better.

At this broadest level, one criteria of quality of service system may be accessibility – how many parents in practice have access to high quality services? Are there sufficient services to permit this? Are they distributed to permit this? Are they offered at a price that permits this? Are the hours of opening and other aspects sufficiently flexible and responsive to the needs of families to permit this?

Placing day care in a broader policy framework

Issues of quality – definition, attainment, accessibility – are clearly key issues for the policy agenda. Other items have also been raised. Even brief consideration, however, makes it obvious that the policy issues on this agenda should not be considered in isolation, but within a broader policy framework encompassing education and child welfare, family policy, community development, equality of opportunity and employment. For example:

- it is increasingly unsatisfactory to treat day care and education separately;

- how the costs of day care should be allocated, and what proportion parents should pay, can only really be discussed in relation to the broader issue of how all the costs of raising children should be divided and allocated;

- defining quality in day care services cannot be done satisfactorily without asking broader questions about childhood – what sort of children do we want? What sort of childhood do we want them to have? What rights do children have?

- discussion about whether or not workplace-attached day care should be encouraged or discouraged involve issues concerning mobility and the cohesion, well-being and importance of local neighbourhoods;

- the provision of day care services and the situation of day care workers, who are predominantly women, should not be divorced from considerations about equality of opportunity for women in employment, or indeed equality of opportunity for children;

- the future role of day care depends not only on developments in the labour market, but also on the development and effectiveness of policies to make employment more responsive to the needs of parents. For example, Swedish day care policies are regarded as part of a system which also includes employment policies providing extensive rights for parents; the introduction in the 1970s of the right for parents to work part-time reduced the time spent by children in day care, while recent extensions of paid Parental Leave have meant children starting day care later. Indeed, this trend to an increasing period of Parental Leave is apparent in other countries too; Germany and France, for example, both offer at least 18 months of leave (though their measures are inferior to the Swedish scheme in several respects, including pay and flexibility). The implications of Parental Leave policy for day care provision are considerable, especially for the care of infants, and it is particularly important that policy in these two areas should be considered within a common framework.

A major challenge for the 1990s therefore is not only the need to prepare a new policy on early childhood services, which incorporates care and education; but to find a way of integrating this into a wider interlocking policy framework. To complicate matters further, policy has to confront the essentially dynamic nature of changes currently underway involving gender, caring work and other forms of work – and the relationship between them. It cannot be emphasised too strongly that the entry of increasing numbers of women into the labour market has major ramifications for caring work, whether it involves children or adults, and for the costs of caring.

A research agenda for the 1990s

The policy agenda therefore is a long one, and little progress has so far been made. What about the research agenda? While the 'Belsky' debate remains one of the main research issues at present, a number of major studies currently underway in this country and the United States should produce relevant findings over the next 5 years. We doubt therefore whether further work on this issue is justified. Instead, we would propose nine main areas where work needs doing:

1. *The identification of further conditions* that facilitate developmentally enhancing experience for children in day care, especially for infants;

2. *The development of indicators of quality* – of care, of service and of service system – which can be used by practitioners at a local level, as well as by researchers;

3. *The development of a national system of monitoring* for quality, staffing and parental usage, demand for and satisfaction with services;

4. *The development of structures and programmes,* including training and other interventions, to improve quality;

5. *Monitoring the workings of the private market and its regulation,* for example the consequences for children, parents, workers and other interested groups of present private market developments, and the development and impact of local authority policy and practice towards the regulation of the private market in the context of the new Children Act;

6. *A survey of the staffing of day care facilities* in the U K, taking as a model (though with appropriate revisions for the British context) the recent U S National Child Care Staffing Study, which not only looks at staffing but relates this to quality of care and children's development;

7. *Detailed study of the needs of certain groups of children* and parents and how adequately these are being met, the groups to include ethnic minorities, rural populations and children with special needs;

8. *Analysis of the costs of day care* and their allocation, and of the implications of different systems of funding and charging;

9. *The integration of care and education at all levels* – national government, local government and in individual institutions – and in all functions – policy, training, administration and practice. It is clear that the distinctions currently operating are artificial and that an integrated system of pre-school provision would better meet the needs of children and parents.

We do not claim that such an agenda is exhaustive; it is put forward as a basis for discussion. There needs to be a process of review and consultation, involving all interested parties, to produce a comprehensive and prioritised research *and* development programme – and it should be recognised and emphasised that the agenda we have just listed is really an agenda for research and development, in which research is closely linked to the development of policy and services. Furthermore, taking this research and development approach, a central feature of any programme should be the building of close relationships between researchers and practitioners, working together regularly both on specific practical issues and problems, locally defined, as well as on longer-term and more general issues and problems.

It must also be apparent that such a programme of research and development will cost a substantial amount. Funding should come from service providers in both the public and private sectors, with additional support from Central Government. The money so raised could then be divided between local funds managed by consortia of researchers and providers of services (and other interested parties), and centrally allocated funds for larger scale, nationally directed work. Current expenditure on R&D on day care (or more broadly, on early childhood services covering both day care and education) represents well under 0.1 per cent of the annual running costs of these services. This level might be increased to 1 per cent within 3 years and 2 per cent within 5 years. Although this would still leave the ratio of R&D expenditure to total service costs well below levels regarded as necessary in private industry, it would enable a major programme of local and national research and development to be introduced, developed and sustained.

Printed in the United Kingdom for HMSO.
Dd.0295236, 10/91, C8, 3390/3, 5673, 167767.